For my father, Jack Brown,
the most supportive dad in the world.

And in memory of my mother, Edith Brown.

Writers' & Artists' Hideouts

Writers' & Artists' Hideouts

GREAT
GETAWAYS
FOR
SEDUCING
THE MUSE

Andrea Brown

SANGER, CALIFORNIA

Printed in the United States of America
Published by Quill Driver Books/Word Dancer Press, Inc.
1831 Industrial Way #101
Sanger, California 93657
559-876-2170 • 1-800-497-4909 • FAX 559-876-2180
QuillDriverBooks.com
Info@QuillDriverBooks.com

Quill Driver Books' titles may be purchased in quantity at special discounts for educational, fund-raising, business, or promotional use. Please contact Special Markets, Quill Driver Books/Word Dancer Press, Inc. at the above address or at 1-800-497-4909.

Quill Driver Books/Word Dancer Press, Inc. project cadre:
Susan Klassen, John David Marion, Stephen Blake Mettee,

First Printing

To order another copy of this book, please call
1-800-497-4909

Library of Congress Cataloging-in-Publication Data

Brown, Andrea.
  Writer's and artist's hideouts : great getaways for seducing the muse / by Andrea Brown.
    p. cm.
  ISBN 1-884956-34-3
  1. Hotels--United States--Guidebooks. 2. Bed and breakfast accommodations--United States--Guidebooks. 3. Creative ability. I. Title.

TX907.2.B78 2004
917.306'2931--dc22

2004005867

Front cover image: The Berwood Hill Inn in Lanesboro, MN. Courtesy Berwood Hill Inn
Back cover image: Richmond Hill Inn, Asheville, NC. Courtesy Richmond Hill Inn

Table of Contents

Acknowledgments

Over the course of two years of working on this book, many people gave me their advice, support, and wisdom, and I am eternally grateful. I especially want to thank my publisher and friend, Steve Mettee, who has more patience than anyone I know. I also thank Susan Klassen who worked long hours to design this book.

And, special thanks to the two wisest women I know, Eleanor Brown and Frances Spiselman, who have always been there for me.

Thanks to all my travel buddies: Christine and Howard Brown, Nancy Ellis, Linda Mead, Rita Rosenkranz, Nadia Reisfeld, Shelly Nerenberg, Barbara and Liza Zimmerman, Beth Laddin, Eileen Gayle, Sandra Beriss, Linda Baker, and Jay Glover.

Many people shared their favorite locales and I must thank Denny and Karen Delk, Elizabeth Pomada and Michael Larsen, Daniel and Leslie Guterman, Lynx Leshinsky, Laura Rennert and Barry Eisler, Ben, Stacie, and Sharon Reisner, Elissa Haden Guest, Jill Kasapligil, Linda Puffenberger, Linda Swingle, Stella Zadeh, David Gersh, Christy Hawes Zatkin, Phyllis and Dr. Barrett Sachs, Katharine Sands, Sharon Manat, Deb and Steve Shear, Elsa Hurley, Toni Stein, Melanie Bragg, Shannon and John Tullius, Robert Wahl, Dee LeRoy, and Dan Poynter.

And, to all the publishers, editors, authors, literary agents, art directors, illustrators, and entertainers who contributed their advice and feedback, my deepest gratitude. Last, but most certainly not least, my love and thanks go to David Spiselman: the best travel buddy, food taster, luggage carrier, technical support, cat caretaker— and the best husband in the world. Sasha and Cassie Cat thank you for taking such good care of them while the creation of this book was in progress. The book wouldn't have gotten finished if not for your wisdom, help, and guidance. You have my deepest gratitude and love.

Introduction

Many of my most memorable life experiences are times when I left the comforts of home, took off by myself, and escaped to a scenic, peaceful place to do some serious thinking or some serious writing.

Solitude can be bliss, but, for myself and many other creative people, it is a necessity. Since I began working in the book publishing business in 1976, I have listened to numerous authors and illustrators complain about working at home—as most writers and artists do. Distractions at home often involve spousal demands, children with needs, pets to feed, ringing phones, chores to finish, refrigerators to raid, and on and on. Even the most disciplined and organized find it a constant challenge. If a writer or artist is under deadline, the pressure can be enormous.

I am lucky enough to have built a career that allows me to indulge in my travel passion. Over the years, I have kept notes and brochures on my favorite places for those times when I needed to decamp to recharge my enthusiasm or to simply get the creative juices flowing.

I often make friends swear they won't divulge the names of some of these prized locations, as I don't want them getting too crowded. But, after hearing more and more writers and artists complain about needing a special place to which they might escape, I decided to share my findings.

That's what this book is, a roster of special places; a guide to the wonderful, the beautiful, the relaxing. In these pages you will find sites that are as good for the eye as they are for the soul, from small cabins and hostels to luxurious hotels—and, I've even included a hotel or motel chain if it meets my criteria.

The book is organized by region. Because of my personal preferences, because some areas are especially scenic and conducive for creative escapes, and because some places tend to have more active writer and artist populations, no attempt has been made to balance the number of entries region to region. Many locations included in this book are not on the beaten path, yet I have tried to narrow the selection to places that are welcoming and safe, especially for women who may be traveling alone. My apologies if your favorite venue is not included. While I have traveled much of the country, there are obviously some places I have not yet discovered.

Since many creative folks don't drive or don't want to waste their energy in travel time, I have included places in major cities that are easy to reach without a car. For instance, if you live in New York City, find it difficult to work at home, and don't want to travel far, I suggest comfortable and reasonable places in Manhattan. It can be especially fun to stay in a hotel in your very own city if only for a change of scenery.

To most of us, price is important so I have coded each location from $ to $$$$$, that is, from inexpensive to quite expensive. I strongly suggest traveling in the off-season, not only to get the best rates possible, but also for true peace and quiet. Go to Colorado's Vail or Aspen areas in the fall or spring, avoiding the winter ski season. Resist Maine in the summer and stay away from southern Florida during the winter months. Most of the places recommended have Web sites, so make a habit of checking the sites for special off-season or package deals.

While this book is primarily a travel guide, each chapter includes tips, advice, and suggestions from publishers, editors, authors, illustrators, literary agents, and art directors to assist you in accomplishing the most during your stolen moments.

Consider alternatives other than those listed in this book as well. There are over 7,000 site listings of vacation home rentals available on the Internet. Extended-stay facilities, intended primarily for business travelers, often have excellent rates for those who will stay for five days or longer. Check out Residence Inns (800-331-313, www.residenceinn.com), Staybridge Suites (800-238-8000, (www.staybridge.com), or ExtendedStay America (800-398-7829, www.extendedstay.com). Or, consider renting a Winnebago or motor home so you have a rolling office that you can pull over and go to work anywhere.

So, let loose! From the rustic Red Fish Lake Lodge in Idaho to a luxurious oceanfront room at the Marriot Wailea-Outrigger Hotel in Maui; from a cabin on an ocean cliff at Lucia Lodge in Big Sur to the Gramercy Park Hotel in New York City, explore your creative self, meet those deadlines, grab some peace of mind, and arrive home refreshed and rejuvenated.

How To Use This Book

This guide is broken down into ten geographical regions. If you have an idea of what area you would like to visit, browse the sites listed in that region. If you know the name of a venue, use the handy index starting on page 257 to find the page number on which it is listed. There is also an index by city starting on page 265.

Addresses, phone numbers, e-mail, and web sites—when available—are provided. Relative rates are listed as follows:

$ = Inexpensive

$$ = Moderate

$$$ = Moderately expensive

$$$$ = Expensive

$$$$$ = Quite Expensive

If a location does not accept credit cards, the listing will say so; otherwise, all the accommodations accept most major credit cards.

Web sites often provide up-to-date information and sometimes offer special rates, so it's a good idea to check them out. Yet, Web site addresses sometimes change. In the few instances where this happens, go to Google.com (www.google.com) and key the venue's phone number, starting with the area code, into the search field. When you click on the search button, Google will give you current links to the venue. If you are reading the Microsoft Reader eBook version of this book, you can click on the venue's link and instantly be connected via the Internet.

The inclusion of a site in this book is on merit only; no payment, complimentary stays, or other remuneration were requested or received. However, when you make reservations, please mention seeing the venue's listing in this book.

PREPARING FOR YOUR TRIP

Whether planning six months or six hours ahead, there are a few things to do to make sure the trip is safe, uneventful (in any negative way), and productive.

1. Make a checklist of everything you need to deal with before leaving. Include things like stopping the mail and newspaper, arranging for pets to be fed and plants to be watered, and posting the pizza delivery number on the refrigerator for your husband.

2. Leave your cell phone number or the number of the place at which you will be staying with a responsible adult. Make sure that he or she understands it is to be used only for bona fide emergencies. If you take your cell phone, don't leave it on all the time. Rather, check for urgent messages two times a day, perhaps at 9 A.M. and 9 P.M. and call home to touch base with your spouse or children once a day.

3. Check the weather forecast in the area of your destination so you'll know what clothes to pack.

4. If you will be driving far, have your car serviced before leaving.

5. Pack one bag for work-related items and a separate bag for clothes and personal items.

WHAT TO PACK

Pack light, but pack intelligently. Clothing that can be "layered" such as tee shirts, sweaters, and light jackets, help cut down on bulk. Make a written list. Here are some things to consider putting:

- A good dictionary and thesaurus
- Your notebook computer or pocket PC
- A printer and plenty of paper
- Scratch pads, notebooks, pens, pencils
- Art supplies
- Camera and film
- Flashlight
- Alarm clock
- Umbrella
- Comfortable walking shoes
- Credit cards
- Cash (not too much) or travelers' checks
- Ear plugs
- Medicines
- Sunglasses
- Your favorite snack foods
- Swim suit (for off hours)
- A good novel (again, for off hours)

Security Tips

Take common sense precautions such as not walking in secluded places after dark and most likely your trip will be tranquil and safe. Single women traveling alone should employ extra safeguards. For instance, when making the reservation, request a room near the office or one that isn't on the ground floor. Here are some additional tips to make your trip memorable for the right reasons:

- Keep a close eye on your luggage.

- Use all the available locks when in your room.

- Most room doors have a peephole device that allows you to see who is at the door. Use it religiously. If the person at the door claims to be a repairman or hotel employee, call the front desk to verify this before opening the door.

- When you arrive in the room, check out the phone so you will be familiar with its use in the case of an emergency.

- Take as few valuables as you can, and store those in the in-room safe or at the front desk when you are out of your room. This goes for your notebook computer, too.

- If you need help, yell "Fire," as some people will ignore pleas for help, but will respond or call 911 if they hear cries of a fire.

- Tell the desk clerk not to announce your room number at check-in.

THE
PACIFIC NORTHWEST

Idaho

Washington

Oregon

Idaho

Idaho is a large and especially long state and close enough for writers and artists from anywhere in the Pacific Northwest to drive to for a few days. Included are places close to Boise, with easy access from Oregon, Utah and California.

Boise

A small but historic and pretty college city with many museums, gardens, parks, magnificent mountain views and probably the only city left in America that does not have grid-locked traffic at 5 P.M. on a Friday afternoon. For writers and artists living in the country, Boise is just big enough to feel like a real city yet small enough to walk around in during afternoon breaks.

Downtown Boise
~Owyhee Plaza Hotel

Conveniently located in the middle of downtown, close to restaurants and shopping, with a pool, room refrigerators, room service, and a restaurant and lounge, TV, air conditioning, modem hook-ups, business center, and one-hundred rooms with desks.While not large, these rooms are big enough to work in comfortably.

> 1109 Main St., Boise, ID 83702
> 800-233-4611
> www.owyheeplaza.com
> $–$$

~Idaho Heritage Inn

This six-room bed and breakfast, located in the former Governor's Mansion offers private baths, local TV, modem hook-ups, full breakfast service, a fax/copier, and quaint air conditioned rooms perfect for a quieter setting than in the downtown area.

> 109 W. Idaho, Boise, ID 83702
> 208-342-8066
> www.idheritageinn.com
> $–$$

~The Northwest Lodge

This new, rustically-elegant inn off I-84, with 17 suites, features wood and stone details throughout. Wine, beer, and cookies and milk are served in a large, warm lobby. The inn has an indoor pool, spa, fitness room, and serves a continental breakfast. Rooms have refrigerators and desks with data ports. Wireless Internet access is available

> 6989 Federal Wy., Boise, ID 83716
> 866-38LODGE
> www.nwlodge.com
> $$

~The Anniversary Inn

Part of a small chain of themed suite hotels (Salt Lake City also has two), this is a wonderful place for creative people, as each of the fourteen rooms has its own unique theme that can really help capture the right mood in which to work. The most unique room in the Boise hotel is the Sleeping Beauty room, complete with a wood-planked entry, turret, and castle walls. You can choose from water to safari settings and the rooms are spacious enough to work in. A most unusual inn and even if you don't stay here, tours of the rooms are available.

> 1575 S. Lusk Ave., Boise, ID 83706
> 877-386-4900
> www.anniversaryinn.com
> $$–$$$

Boise Airport

~Best Western Vista Inn

This chain motel which feels more like a safe hotel has indoor lobbies, halls and 87 comfortable rooms facing inside, an indoor heated pool/spa, a fitness room, and serves a large continental breakfast. It also affords all of the usual large chain amenities.

> 2645 Airport Wy., Boise, ID 83705
> 800-727-5006, 208-336-8100
> $–$$

Suburban Boise

Caldwell

~Wild Rose Manor

A bed and breakfast with three themed rooms, hot tubs, air conditioning, coffee, and a full breakfast.

> 5800 Oasis Rd., Caldwell, ID 83605
> 208-454-3331
> www.wildrosemanor
> $$–$$$

WRITING WITH THE PEN OF MY LIFE

When I go away to write, I go somewhere my heart yearns to see or where I feel I will be in virgin territory, so it becomes more of a pilgrimage. I always take little spiral hardcover notebooks that I can fold back and hold in the palm of my hand to easily and immediately take notes or write down phrases. The phrases or notes are like written photographs that, when I look at them, vividly return me to the moment.

I usually go away for two weeks, fill at least one notebook, and then, at home, I spend the next month writing from the notes, while my impressions are immediate. I write what I saw in that moment in the universe or in my heart, and hope that it might mean something to other people. I hope to create some universality that says I am not so different from anyone else.

I can only write from my own experience, or as my editor Mitch Horowitz at Penguin says, "You are writing with the pen of your life."

It wouldn't seem right to go away to a beautiful place in the country, if as a writer, you have nothing to say. If you have nothing to say, why would anyone want to read what you write. Keep your antennae and heart open, have something to say, and then write about it.

—*Toinette Lippe, Publisher of Bell Tower Books (Random House) and author of* Nothing Left Over: A Plain and Simple Life *and* Caught in the Act: Reflections on Being, Knowing and Doing.

Central Southern Idaho

McCall: About 100 miles north of Boise
~Hotel McCall

Overlooking Payette Lake, this small European-style inn has some rooms with lake and mountain views. Newer rooms include kitchenettes. The hotel itself has a fabulous dinner` restaurant and breakfast is served there for guests. There is also a wine hour and cookies and milk are served in the evening in a library perfect that is perfect for writing. The original rooms in the hotel, built in 1904, are small and basic but with desks and good lighting. Amenities include private baths, cable TV, telephones with data ports, and coffee and tea are available all day. Newer rooms have air conditioning, Jacuzzi tubs, and some balconies (elevator too). Ask for one of the two front rooms overlooking the lake as they are bigger. The quaint town of McCall is right outside the front door and is perfect for walking around during breaks.

> 1101 N. 3rd St., McCall, ID 83638
> 866-800-1183
> www.mccall-idchamber.org
> $–$$$$

~Bear Creek Lodge

This lovely, wood lodge is tucked into 65 acres of hills and woods near Payette Lake and is ideal for people wanting a small, quiet getaway spot just outside town. There are cabins as well as rooms in the lodge complete with refrigerators, microwaves, coffee, and data ports. Also, there is an outdoor spa, pretty decks, and a fitness room overlooking the creek. Closed winters.

> P.O. Box 970, McCall, ID 83638
> 208-634-3551
> www.bearcreeklodge.com.
> $$–$$$

Stanley
~Redfish Lake Lodge

Located inside a state park overlooking the magnificent Redfish Lake, there are cabins and rooms in the lodge itself. The views from the rooms on the second floor of the lodge compensate for the not so fancy rooms. The cabins are much roomier but don't really have a lake view. There is a restaurant, mini-mart, and bar except in the off-season (winter and fall).

Box 9, Stanley, ID 83278
208-774-3536
www.redfishlake.com
$-$$$

~Meadow Creek Inn and Spa

There are six rooms most with mountain views near two rivers and two highways. This is a quiet, peaceful setting, but it is out in the middle of nowhere and only suggested if you really want to get away from it all and have few distractions. Fax/copier, hot tub, sauna, steam rooms, refrigerator and lounge are available.

P.O. Box 43, Stanley, ID 83278
800-811-5745
www.meadowcreekinn.com
$-$$$$

Kamiah

~Hearthstone Lodge

In North central Idaho, on the historic Lewis and Clark Trail and overlooking the Clearwater River, sits this 6-unit lodge. There are 29 acres of woods surrounding the inn, as well as river activities. The rooms and two cottages have fireplaces, cathedral ceilings, spa tubs, canopy beds, robes, private baths, balconies – some with river views—and a full breakfast is included in the price of the room. The common rooms contain beautiful antique furnishings and there is a well-stocked library.

Box 1492, Kamiah, ID 83536
208-935-1492 or 877-LODGE4U (reservations only)
www.hearthstone-lodge.com
$$-$$$$$

Hayden Lake
~The Clark House on Hayden Lake

This mansion, originally a private summer home and the most expensive home in Idaho, was renovated in 1989 as an inn.

On the National Register of Historic Places, the inn has ten rooms on over twelve acres of grounds overlooking beautiful Hayden Lake. Rooms have private baths, king or queen feather beds, and antique furnishings. Some rooms have fireplaces and large tubs. Rooms range from cozy and small to elegant suites with breakfast included. There are also gourmet six-course dinners at the inn's restaurant for about $50 per person.

> 5250 E. Hayden Lake Rd., Hayden Lake, ID 83835.
> 800-765-4593, 208-772-3470
> www.Clarkhouse.com.
> **$$–$$$$$**

Sun Valley

Ketchum
~Tamarack Lodge

This European-styled inn, located in the heart of downtown Ketchum in Sun Valley, is kind of a mix between a hotel and motel. There are 26 large guest rooms . All rooms have refrigerators, microwave ovens, coffee makers, hair dryers, desks or tables, cable TV, air-conditioning and modem hook-ups. Some rooms have mountain views. Suites have separate bedrooms. The inn has an indoor pool and spa.

> 291 Walnut Ave., N., Ketchum, ID 83353
> 800-521-5379
> www.tamaracksunvalley.com
> **$–$$$$**

Sun Valley
~Sun Valley Resort

This is a large hotel with a cozy feeling. During non-peak ski season, the resort feels quiet and serene. Magnificent mountains surround the main lodge, built in 1937. The main lodge is where we suggest you stay, although there are also condominiums and cottages on the grounds. The Old World charm is combined with elegant touches in the rooms. Restaurants are located in the lodge and in the shopping area next to the hotel. There are some diversions like a pool, hot tub and fitness room. The wood-paneled lounge is a wonderful place to work in during off-hours. One of the few large resorts recommended for creative types in this book.

One Sun Valley Rd., Box 10, Sun Valley, ID 83353
800-786-8259
www.sunvalley.com
$–$$$$$

Sun Valley Lodge, Sun Valley, ID. Rustic elegance can be found high up in the mountains at this full-service hotel that manages to also feel intimate and cozy, especially in non-skiing season. Courtesy of Sun Valley Resort

Hailey

~Wood River Inn

This is the area's newest motel/inn, with 56 large rooms in the quaint, quiet town of Hailey, far enough from the ski action in Sun Valley but actually only ten miles away. Some rooms have kitchens, Jacuzzi tubs and fireplaces and TV, and all have refrigerators, coffee, air conditioning and external phone jacks. The inn has a heated indoor pool and a spa and breakfast is included.

> 603 N. Main St., Hailey, ID 83333
> 877-542-0600
> www.woodriverinn.com
> $$

Salmon River Country

Riggins

~Salmon Rapids Lodge

Nicer than most motels, This Best-Western lodge has 55 rooms with terraces overlooking the Salmon River. The lodge also has a pool, spa, fitness room, modem hook-ups, and a fax/copier. Breakfast is included.

> Box 408, 1010 S. Main St. Riggins, ID 83549
> 877-957-2743
> www.salmonrapids.com
> $-$$$

Washington

The state of Washington is one of the greenest states in the country. It is also hard to turn around without hitting water or seeing a snow-covered volcano or mountain loom in the distance. Because of this, Washington is a beautiful and serene place for writers and artists.

From the Tacoma/Seattle area there are a number of choices, depending on whether you want more mountains or more trees and water. Heading north from Seattle, one highly recommended area is the San Juan Islands, but it takes several hours to get there from Seattle via the Washington State

Ferry system. The phone number for ferry information is 800-843-3779 inside Washington; outside of Washington state, dial 206-464-6400.

San Juan Islands

Orcas Island

Orcas Island, also called the "Emerald Isle and Horseshoe Island" because of its shape, is not named for the whales, but in honor of a Spanish viceroy in Mexico. One must-see visit is to Mount Constitution which offers a view of all the islands, the waters of Puget Sound, and Mount Baker.

Olga
~Spring Bay Inn B & B

This is the only inn we have ever seen that includes a two-hour kayaking trip as part of the room price. Hidden down a private dirt road, this beautiful inn has 5 rooms, but ask for the ones upstairs with the private decks overlooking the sound, or the downstairs room that has a sitting area by the window—perfect for writers and artists for light and view—as well as a private deck. All rooms have lovely bathrooms, robes, and fireplaces. There is a private beach with a spa and about 137 acres of woods surrounding the building. Breakfast, before the kayak trip is followed by a gourmet brunch and both are included in the price of the room.

P.O. Box 97, Olga, WA 98279
360-376-5531
www.Springbayinn.com
$$$$–$$$$$

Spring Bay Inn, Olga, WA. Owned by two former forest rangers, this bed and breakfast also offers two free hours of supervised kayaking on Puget Sound. Courtesy of Matt Clark

Deer Harbor
~The Inn on Orcas Island

Suites and cottages nestled on pleasantly landscaped hill overlooking the harbor and Puget sound make this a relaxing location away from the main town and ferry. Some rooms have jetted tubs and fireplaces and all have balconies with water views.

> P.O. Box 309, Deer Harbor, WA 98243
> 888-886-1661
> www.Deerharborinn.com
> $$–$$$$

~The Resort at Deer Harbor

Overlooking the beachfront and marina, the resort offers rooms and cottages with private decks and spas, a pool, fireplaces, refrigerators, coffee, microwaves and an on-site restaurant. The resort is located on a hill and the grounds are pleasant and well-maintained.

> 31 Jack and Jill Ln., Deer Harbor, WA 98243
> 888-376-4480
> www.Deerharbor.com
> $$$$–$$$$$

The Resort at Deer Harbor, Deer Harbor, WA. An 80-minute ferry ride through the San Juan Islands of Puget Sound brings you to Orcas Island, the largest and most diverse of the San Juan Islands chain. Courtesy of The Resort at Deer Harbor

Orcas

~Orcas Hotel

The Orcas Hotel affords the easiest accommodations, if you have no car, as this inn is located just opposite the ferry landing for people liking some hustle and bustle. This Victorian inn has twelve rooms, some with water views, jetted tubs, and private balconies and breakfast is included in the inn's restaurant and bar.

> P.O. Box 369, Orcas, WA98280
> 888-672-2792
> www.Orcashotel.com
> $–$$$$

Eastsound

The main town of the island has many shops and restaurants.

~Outlook Inn

This turn-of-the-century hotel is conveniently located right in the heart of the town, but has rooms with beautiful views of the bay surrounded by green, lush hills. There are also sixteen new deluxe suites, or you can take an older room with a shared bath to save money. The inn has a restaurant, but many other dining places are within walking distance.

> P.O. Box 210, Eastsound WA 98245
> 888-OUT-LOOK
> www.outlookinn.com
> $$–$$$$$

~Inn at Ship Bay

Located just outside of town, this inn has one of the best views on the island as it is on the waterfront of Eastsound Bay. The inn has eight acres of lovely grounds with a pond and gardens. There are eleven rooms with king-sized beds, fireplaces, decks with views, as well as an excellent restaurant on the premises.

> 326 Olga Rd., Eastsound, WA 98245
> 877-276-7296
> www.innatshipbay.com
> $$$$–$$$$$

San Juan Island

This island is known as the "Pig War Island," due to a dispute in 1859, when an American settler killed a British-owned boar and started a dispute between the two countries. In 1872, Kaiser Wilhelm of Germany declared that the islands were within the boundaries of the United States. There are many historic buildings, parks and harbor towns with shops and restaurants for small diversions. This is the kind of place you may want to visit during the off-season or on a weekday when, since reservations shouldn't be required, you can drive around and discover a place that strikes you as perfect for working and relaxing, as there are numerous places to stay.

Friday Harbor
~Wayfarer's Rest
One of the most inexpensive places in the Islands to stay, this hostel has fifteen beds with a dorm rate of only $22 per night. Private rooms with kitchen facilities are $55 a night. The Inn is locate right in town.

> 35 Malcolm St., Friday Harbor, WA 98250
> 360-378-6428
> www.rockisland.com/~wayfarersrest/
> $

~Lakedale Resort/Log Cottages
This is an 82-acre resort with a rustic, wood design. The ten rooms in the lodge have private view decks, fireplaces, spa tubs, wetbars, and a continental breakfast is included. The cottages have two bedrooms. Lake swimming is available. Pets are allowed in cottages.

> 4313 Roche Harbor Rd., Friday Harbor, WA 98250
> 800-617-2267
> www.lakedale.com
> $$$$–$$$$$

~San Juan Inn B&B
This Victorian inn, built in 1873, is located near the ferry landing, so no car is necessary. There are nine queen or double rooms, some with shared bath. Two suites have spa tubs but there is an outdoor spa. A large continental breakfast is included.

P.O. Box 776, Friday Harbor, WA 98250
800-742-8210
www.sanjuaninn.com
$–$$$$$

~Trumpeter Inn B& B

About 1½ miles from town, this inn has over five acres of gardens, a trout pond and views of False Bay and the Olympic mountains. The five suites have private baths, fireplaces, and private view decks. There is a garden spa and breakfast is included.

318 Trumpeter Wy., Friday Harbor, WA 98250
800-826-7926
www.trumpeterinn.com
$$–$$$$

Whidbey Island

This is the largest island in the United States and it is the entry point via ferry to the San Juan Islands from Anacortes at the northern tip of the island. There are several quaint towns here, with lovely parks and many types of accommodations. The climate is relatively mild on Whidbey even in the winter. Having a car is helpful.

Anacortes

~Sunset Beach B& B

The rooms here have wonderful views of the San Juan Islands. The rooms all have queen beds, private baths, and hot tubs. The price also includes a large breakfast.

2420 Puget Wy., Anacortes, WA 98221
800-359-3448
www.sunsetbeachanacortes.com
$$–$$$

~Islands Inn

This is an upscale motel with 36 rooms, and the fireplace rooms have views of the water, king beds, whirlpool tubs, wet bars and sitting areas perfect for writing and reading. Breakfast is a treat as it is a Dutch breakfast with eggs, ham, and Dutch cheeses, bread, and beverages all inclusive.

> 3401 Commercial Ave., Anacortes, WA 98221
> 866-331-3328
> www.islandsinn.com
> $

Coupeville
~Anchorage Inn

This lovely, 1860s, Victorian bed and breakfast, located in the historic town of Coupeville, has seven warmly decorated rooms with queen or king beds, private baths, and some have wonderful views of the sound. The large wraparound porch also has views of the water and is perfect for just sitting and writing or drawing.

> 807 N. Main St., Coupeville, WA 98239
> 877-230-1313
> www.Anchorage-inn.com
> $–$$$

~The Captain Whidbey Inn

On the bay at Penn Cove, this 32-room inn has accommodated visitors since 1907. The inn's rooms have shared baths, but there are also cottages and cabins on the expansive grounds with private baths and decks. Cabin rooms have fireplaces. The rooms have a bit rustic quality and some are dark, so be sure to ask for a room with a lot of light. There is an outdoor spa. Breakfast is included and the restaurant's view and food (especially dishes with Penn Cove mussels) are popular with locals.

> 2072 W. Captain Whidbey Inn Rd., Coupeville, WA 98239.
> 800-366-4097
> www.captainwhidbey.com
> $–$$$$$

Langley
~Country Cottage of Langley

This small inn has separate and duo cottages, beautiful gardens and water views, and it is a short walk to the downtown shops and restaurants in

Captain Whidbey Inn, Coupeville, WA. Surrounding the inn's buildings are gardens filled with the fresh flowers, produce, and herbs served in the inn's fine restaurant. Courtesy of Captain Whidbey Inn

Langley, the nicest town on the island. Most rooms have fireplaces, TV, and private decks and some have spa tubs. Rooms have refrigerators, coffee, and tables to work at, with views. Breakfast is brought to your room and includes enough food to provide lunch too.

215 Sixth St., Langley, WA 98260
800-713-3860
www.acountrycottage.com
$$$–$$$$

~The Inn at Langley

This luxurious inn, built into a bluff, has 24 rooms with 180-degree waterfront views of the Saratoga Passage of Puget Sound. Rooms have fireplaces, upscale modern furnishings, TV, and whirlpool baths. Their restaurant boasts a renowned chef. The rooms are peaceful and elegant, with lots of natural wood throughout.

> 400 First St., Langley, WA 98260
> 360-221-3033
> www.innatlangley.com
> $$$$$

~Saratoga Inn

One of the fine hotels owned by the Four Sisters Inns, this 15-room stone and wood inn has a wraparound porch overlooking the water, as do most of the rooms. Private, luxurious baths grace each individually decorated room, which also include fireplaces, TV, and many amenities. Gourmet breakfast and wine are served each day.

> 201 Cascade Ave., Langley, WA 98260
> 800-698-2910
> www. foursisters.com
> $$–$$$$$

Olympic Peninsula

The Olympic Peninsula is easily accessed from Seattle via the Edmonds ferry or via Whidbey's Keystone ferry, and much of the peninsula has a relatively moderate climate.

Port Townsend

~The Commander's Beach House

This seaside mansion was originally built in 1934 as the residence of the Commanding Medical Officer of the U.S. Quarantine Station at Point Hudson. The included full breakfast is served on the covered porch, and some of the four rooms have fireplaces and views of the water or mountains. The bed and breakfast is located right at the marina and it is a short walk to the shops and restaurants in town.

> 400 Hudson St., Port Townsend, WA 98368
> 888-385-1778
> www.commandersbeachhouse.com
> $$–$$$$

RELAXATION = PRODUCTIVITY

Living in the Pacific Northwest, come about February or March when there is mold everywhere and it's hard to manage dealing with any more rain, I go off on a yoga retreat or to someplace warm, but I always cleverly include research on a book so I can write the trip off legitimately.

When I illustrated *The Precious Gift*, I had to research bugs so I went to a retreat in Fairfield, Iowa and during breaks took out a butterfly net to research insects. If you are going to deduct expenses, it's important to fine-tune your time and document the time spent working carefully. Some states allow freelancers to write off a certain amount of time when they do work on trips and artists should check with their accountants to find out how much can be legally written off. Document the time. Keep impeccable records. I take photographs to help document the work accomplished. Creative people should always combine work with some "R and R" time—the more relaxed I am, the better my work gets and the more productive I am. In this crazy and frantic world, try to take ten days minimum. And you have to stay in places that are aesthetically pleasing and relaxing, with views that are inspiring. I really like quiet places where the sky is pitch black at night and you can see the stars. Don't just get in the car and drive. Research places. Go on the Internet.

Sometimes I go with other artists to split expenses. We'll make a plan like rising at 5 A.M. to work, meet for lunch and a walk or some other break of some kind, then work again and meet for dinner together.

A full day before you go, thoughtfully pack for the trip. You can't expect to drive around to find supplies. Bring all the stuff you need. I prepare sketches ahead and bring a board to paint on but keep it simple. Take material for only the paintings you know you will work on.

And, you must be ruthless. This is your quiet time. No one can call or disturb you. Only you can call family. Sometimes, when money is tight, I simply stay at a friend's house. Some of my friends have fabulous vacation houses and when they aren't using them, they are happy to have someone at the house. I always leave them a painting or a sketch as a thank you gift.

—*Woodleigh Marx Hubbard, author/illustrator of* Hip Cat, C Is For Curious, The Friendship Book, For the Love of a Pug *and many other children's and gift books. She is also the creator of a jewelry line called "Grin and Wear It."*

~The James House

This lovely Victorian mansion perches on top of a bluff overlooking the water just a couple of blocks from the main business district of town. There are ten rooms and a cottage, with fireplaces, TV, data ports, and phones, and breakfast and snacks are served.

> 1238 Washington St., Port Townsend, WA 98368
> 800-385-1238
> www.jameshouse.com
> $$–$$$$

Bainbridge Island

~Fuurin-Oka Futon & Breakfast

This traditional Japanese house, tranquil and serene with Japanese gardens, is a wonderful retreat for writers and artists. There is a full Japanese breakfast and the rooms have kitchenettes. Japanese baths, views of the mountains, and a vegetarian-friendly menu round out the place.

> 12580 Vista Dr. NE, Bainbridge Island, WA 98110
> 206-842-4916
> www.futonandbreakfast.com
> $$$

~Gayle Bard's Old Mill Guest House

A perfect spot for artists, as this private guest house is owned by a renowned Northwest artist and has art throughout the house and gardens, as well as a library, patio, and gardens to relax and work in.

> 6159 Old Mill Rd., Bainbridge Island, WA 98110
> 206-842-8543
> www.oldmillguesthouse.com
> $$$

Poulsbo

~The Moore House

Just north of Bainbridge Island, this one-bedroom suite with kitchenette has its own entrance into a charming old house, with spectacular views of Liberty Bay from the private deck.

19589 Front St., Poulsbo, WA 98370
360-598-3500
www.themoorehouseonline.com
$$–$$$$

Seattle

~The Edgewater Inn

Located right on pier 67, this is Seattle's only hotel directly on the waterfront, with great views of Puget Sound. The location is perfect for walking around and has many good seafood restaurants nearby. It has all the amenities of a large hotel and looks a bit like a ship, with mountain lodge décor in its 200-plus rooms.

2411 Alaskan Wy., Seattle, WA 98121
800-624-0670
www.Edgewaterhotel.com
$$$–$$$$

~The Sorrento Hotel

Located on Fist Hill above downtown Seattle, this historic hotel was designed in 1908 to resemble an Italian villa and has 76 rooms and suites with private baths. Amenities include data ports and in-room fax machines, and bed warmers, as well as a fitness center for guests and a gourmet restaurant.

900 Madison St., Seattle, WA 98104
206-622-6400
www.slh.com/Sorrento/
$$$$–$$$$$

~Bacon Mansion

This is a bed and breakfast in the historic district of Seattle, two blocks away from the Broadway shopping area. This mansion has a grand staircase, a turn-of-the century library, and breakfast is served in the formal dining room. Most of the eleven rooms have private baths, and all have TV and phones.

959 Broadway E., Seattle, WA 98102
800-240-1864

www.Baconmansion.com
$$–$$$$

~Inn at Queen Anne

Located next to the Seattle Center and Space Needle, this charming inn has 68 quaint rooms, some with views, kitchenettes and beautiful gardens. There is complimentary breakfast and on some evenings wine is served.

505 First Ave. N., Seattle, WA 98109
800-952-5043
www.innatqueenanne.com
$$–$$$

~The Paramount Hotel

This is a charming 146-room hotel near the Convention Center, with elegance and style and all the amenities of a nice hotel.

724 Pine St., Seattle, WA 98101
800-325-4000
www.Paramounthotelseattle.com
$$$–$$$$

JUST START WRITING

When I sold my first book, *Suffer the Children,* in 1977, based on a proposal, Helen Meyer, the publisher at Dell Publishing Company, told me she wanted the entire manuscript in thirty days.

Whenever I start a book, I always think it's absurd that I can write a book, and that no one, certainly not me, can write a 500-page novel. But I know I can write 15 pages every day, so eventually I'll have 500 of them.

I just started writing and got that first book done on deadline. Then, Helen asked me to write a second book in another thirty days.

—*John Saul, author of thirty bestselling novels including* Suffer the Children, Black Lightning *and* The Blackstone Chronicles. *His latest novel,* Midnight Voices *is in film development with Steven Soderbergh and George Clooney. John Saul lives in Washington state.*

~Hostelling International-Seattle

This is an inexpensive and nice hostel experience at a great location near Pike Place Market, with individual and group accommodations for as many as190 people available. There is a lounge, library, and self-service kitchen. Credit cards are accepted.

> 84 Union St., Seattle, WA 98101
> 888-622-5443
> www.hiseattle.org
> $

In the Cascade Mountains and Outside of Seattle

Lummi Island

~Willows Inn

Take a ferry from Bellingham, Washington for a magnificent view of the San Juan Islands from this old farm inn built on a hill, with 8 rooms with private entrances. The rooms are cozy with fireplaces and there is also a cottage and guest house with spa tubs. A full farm-style breakfast is included featuring organic products, and the restaurant at the inn also serves dinners. This spot is secluded and peaceful. Bike rentals are available for use during work breaks. Winter rates are low and a great time to watch storms roll in from the ocean and sound.

> 2579 W. Shore Dr., Lummi Island, WA 98262
> 888-294-2620
> www.willows-inn.com
> $–$$$$$

Snoqualmie

~Salish Lodge and Spa

Only 30 minutes away from Seattle but atop the magnificent 268-foot Snoqualmie Falls, this lodge has 89 rooms, all with fireplaces, whirlpool baths, and elegant furnishings. Large country breakfasts are served and there are spa treatments, exercise facilities, and beautiful views. Rated by Conde' Nast Traveler's gold list as one of the best places to stay in the world.

6501 Railroad Ave. SE, Snoqualmie, WA 98065
800-826-6124
www.salishlodge.com
$$$$

Leavenworth
~Mountain Home Lodge

On a spectacular site in the Washington Cascades, the lodge has ten guest rooms and two cottages, all with handmade quilts and maple furniture. Rooms have CD stereos, binoculars, coffee, robes, and port wine. Facilities include a heated pool, tennis courts, spa, and over 40 miles of trails to walk during work breaks. The area is snowy in winter. Breakfast is included and the inn's restaurant is highly rated for its gourmet dinners. Many activities are available but this is also a peaceful and serene setting for solitude. Rates are lower in summer.

8201 Mountain Home Rd., Leavenworth, WA, 98826
800-414-2378
www.mthome.com
$$$–$$$$$

Mountain Home Lodge, Leavenworth, WA. High up in the Cascades, the restaurant at this inn is well-known for its innovative Pacific Northwest cuisine. Courtesy of Mountain Home Lodge

Spokane
~Fotheringham House Bed & Breakfast
Beautifully restored, this Queen Anne Victorian house has four rooms, some with shared bathrooms, all on the second floor. Rooms have air conditioning, quilts, and antiques and breakfast is served.

> 2128 W. Second Ave., Spokane, WA 99204
> 509-838-1891
> www.fotheringham.net
> $–$$

~The Davenport Hotel
This historic building in Spokane's downtown was originally built in 1914 but was totally renovated in 2002. There are 284 beautifully decorated rooms with pine and mahogany furniture, Irish linens, robes, private bathrooms with marble showers, and high-speed Internet access with triple line phones. Pets are allowed and there are restaurants in the hotel and nearby.

> 10 S. Post St. Spokane, WA 99201
> 800-899-1482
> www.Thedavenporthotel.com
> $$–$$$$

The Washington Coast

The Ocean Shores area on the coast is a three-hour drive from both Seattle and Portland, Oregon.

Moclips
~Ocean Crest Resort
The studios and suites that have magnificent ocean vistas also have fireplaces and kitchenettes. There is a recreation center with indoor pool, spa and other facilities, and the best time to come here is in the off-season during winter when dramatic storms roll in from the Pacific Ocean.

> 4651 SR 109, P.O. Box 7, Moclips, WA 98562
> 800-684-6439
> www.oceancrestresort.com
> $–$$

Oregon

Portland

From Portland, it is only a matter of hours west to the ocean, or east to the mountains and high desert or south to the Ashland-Medford area.

~Heron Haus

An English Tudor-style inn, this quiet and beautiful retreat has six rooms with DSL ports, radios, fireplaces, hardwood floors and most of the rooms have mountain or city views. The Nob Hill neighborhood has restaurants and boutique shops. Breakfast is included.

> 2545 NW Westover Rd., Portland, OR 97210
> 503-274-1846
> www.heronhaus.com
> $$–$$$

~The Heathman Hotel

This is a well-known, historic hotel in downtown Portland with 150 rooms and all the amenities of a luxury hotel including marble in the bathrooms. Many celebrities stay here and the library has signed copies of books by authors who have stayed as guests. It is a ten-story building with an excellent restaurant although there is an extra charge for parking.

> 1001 SW Broadway, Portland, OR 97205
> 800-551-0011, 503-241-4100
> www.Heathmanhotel.com
> $$$–$$$$$

~Mallory Hotel

Located in a quiet location between the northwest district and downtown, this historic hotel has 130 rooms and a warm, traditional feel, yet it offers full business services. Rooms have oak furniture and floral-print décor, TV, irons, safes and other hotel amenities. There are some suites available and the lobby has elaborate chandeliers, leaded glass skylights, and a grandfather clock. There is an elegant marble-pillared dining room on the premises.

729 SW 15th, Portland, OR 97205
800-228-8657
www.malloryhotel.com
$$

Willamette Valley

Eugene
~Campbell House Inn

They call this 19-room Victorian estate built in 1892 "A City Inn." It is located two blocks from downtown Eugene and near the university. There are also suites, a cottage, and magnificent gardens with a gazebo. Some rooms have fireplaces and whirlpool baths but all have private bathrooms. All the rooms have luxurious amenities and high-speed Internet access. A full breakfast is included. The public rooms downstairs have nooks perfect for curling up with a good book. It is listed as one of the top "American Historic Inns" in the country.

252 Pearl St., Eugene, OR 97401
800-264-2519
www.campbellhouse.com
$–$$$$$

Cascade Mountains

Steamboat
~Steamboat Inn

Located about two hours from Eugene or Medford and 38 miles east of Roseburg off Highway 138, this 19-room inn offers suites with fireplaces, air conditioning, decks with views of the North Umpqua River, as well as pine-paneled cabins with kitchenettes, gas stoves, and hand-quilted comforters. Some cabins have river views and all have private baths. The inn also has a gourmet restaurant on the premises, and a library perfect for working and reading. Closed January–February.

42705 North Umpqua Hwy., Steamboat, OR 97447
800-840-8825

www.thesteamboatinn.com
$$-$$$$

Southern Oregon

The Rogue River area in southern Oregon is easily reached from California via Interstate 5 and from all parts of Oregon, and the towns of Ashland, Jacksonville and Medford are wonderful places to walk around during breaks from writing or painting. Ashland is home to the Oregon Shakespeare Festival so it is a perfect hideaway for writers.

Ashland
~Stratford Inn

There are 53 deluxe rooms at this inn, close to the theatre, with refrigerators, kitchenettes, coffee, TV, air conditioning, and the inn has an indoor pool, spa and sundeck.

555 Siskiyou Blvd., Ashland, OR 97520
800-547-4741
www.stratfordinnashland.com
$-$$

~Arden Forest Inn

A quiet bed and breakfast with a library of over 800 volumes and artworks, owned by a theatre historian and designer who loves to discuss literature. Some rooms have a view, and all rooms have high-speed Internet access. A full breakfast is served.

261 W. Hersey, Ashland, OR 97520
541-488-1496
www.afinn.com
$-$$$$

~Winchester Inn

This Victorian inn is built on a hillside, with magnificent English gardens and gazebos on the grounds that give it a fairyland feel. The sixteen rooms and suites are a mix of Victorian charm and all the modern amenities travelers need, such as TV, private baths with spa tubs, fireplaces, balconies, phones, data ports, and full breakfast and treats are included. It is a short walk to town.

> 35 S. Second St., Ashland, OR 97520
> 800-972-4991
> www.winchesterinn.com
> **$$$–$$$$**

~The Woods House

This six-room Craftsman inn has private baths, air conditioning, lots of books in its library, fresh cookies, and breakfast in the lovely garden.

> 333 N. Main St. Ashland, OR 97520
> 800-435-8260, 541-488-1598
> www.Woodshouse.com
> **$$–$$$**

~AYH- Hostel

As with most hostels, there are group rooms and single, private rooms, but prices begin at $13 per night and there is a kitchen and common rooms. Located close to town and the theatre, it is a great spot for budget-minded artists and writers.

> 150 N. Main St. Ashland, OR 97520
> 541-482-9217
> www.ashlandhostel.com
> **$**

Jacksonville
~McCully House Inn

This is a Gothic revival mansion built in 1861 in this historic town, now elegantly restored as a restaurant and inn. The three guest rooms have hardwood floors, private baths, oriental rugs, air conditioning, and antique furnishings. A large breakfast is included and the gourmet restaurant is one of the best in the state. The garden features over 250 roses.

> 240 E. California St., Jacksonville, OR 97530
> 800-367-1942, 541-899-1942

www.McCullyhouseinn.com
$$

Medford

~Under the Greenwood Tree B & B Farm

Unusual rooms with Chippendale furniture and Persian rugs and lower rates for singles make this inn an attractive spot for writers and artists. On an old country estate with a barn, gardens, and an orchard. Tea and sherry are served, as well as breakfast.

3045 Bellinger Ln., Medford, OR 97501
800-766-8099
www.greenwoodtree.com
$$–$$$

Eastern Oregon

Ontario

~Creek House B & B Inn

Located in eastern Oregon on the border of Idaho, just one hour from Boise, this charming house was built in 1908 and is listed on the National Register of Historic Places as the Blackaby House. Oregon pioneer, J.R. Blackaby built it in Queen Anne style. There is a lot of oak paneling and the rooms have quilts, antiques, and telephones. TVs and faxes are available on request. There are four rooms with private bathrooms and many have original light fixtures. The inn is located in a quiet neighborhood with a big porch to sit on.

717 SW 2nd St., Ontario, OR 97914
541-823-0717
www.creekshouse.com
$

Columbia River Gorge Area

Hood River

~Columbia Gorge Hotel

Featuring a spectacular mountain-top location above the Columbia River only an hour east of Portland, this 40-room, historic "country inn" has beautiful gardens surrounding it on three sides as well as views of the hotel of the cliffs and river below from the bar and restaurant in the back. The rooms are a bit small, but cozy enough, with all the amenities of an upscale hotel, and many places to write. The restaurant is famous for its fine cuisine. The hotel is romantic and soothing, but also a lovely spot for women traveling alone.

4000 Westcliff Dr., Hood River, OR 97031
800-345-1921
www.Columbiagorgehotel.com
$$$–$$$$$

~Best Western Hood River Inn

This motel sits directly above the Columbia River, so ask for a room with a river and bridge view and you will forget that you are at a chain motel. Rooms are standard motel rooms with private baths, TV, phone, etc., but there is a pool and a good restaurant with river views. The motel is situated right by the marina and near the shops and restaurants in town.

1108 E. Marina Wy., Hood River, OR 97031
800-828-7873
www.hoodriverinn.com
$–$$$

Oregon Coast

The area includes hundreds of miles of fabulous coastline and many kinds of places to stay, but our listings will focus on the smaller, quaint towns and most serene spots along this famous and dramatic stretch of the country.

Newport

~Sylvia Beach Hotel

Located at the center of the Oregon coast, this small hotel is a must for writers and book lovers, as each of the twenty rooms has a literary theme, such as the Dr. Seuss room, Oscar Wilde room, Mark Twain room, Tennessee Williams room with "STELL-A" on its door, and the Emily Dickinson room, with a beautiful antique writing desk. Built on top of a bluff overlooking the ocean, this inn has no TV's, radios, or telephones in the rooms, so the waves crashing outside your room are the only distractions during your stay here. A full breakfast is served downstairs in the "Table of Contents" room.

267 NW Cliff St. Newport, OR 97365
888-SYLVIAB
www.sylviabeachhotel.com
$–$$$

Oceanside
~House on the Hill Motel (Clifftop Inn)
Located on the northern coast, at the top of a large cliff jutting out into the ocean, this is one of the most stunning spots for a motel in the entire country. This is an unassuming motel, except for utterly spectacular ocean views. Many of the sixteen units include kitchens and all have private bathrooms, TV, coffee, and the usual amenities. Ask for one of the rooms directly above the top of the cliff and be sure to be there for sunset.

1816 Maxwell Mountain Rd., Oceanside, OR 97134
866-CLIFFTOP
www.houseonthehillmotel.com
$$–$$$$

Cannon Beach
~Cannon Beach Hotel
Also on the north coast of Oregon, this small, historic European-style hotel is a short walk to the beach, shops and restaurants of this quaint town. Lodging includes rooms, or bed and breakfast style accommodations, and some rooms have fireplaces, whirlpool tubs, patios or decks, kitchenettes, and all have private bathrooms. No pets or smoking are allowed.

1116 S. Hemlock, Cannon Beach, OR 97110
800-238-4107
www.oregoncoastlodgings.com
$–$$$

Astoria
~Rosebriar Hotel
At the border of Oregon and Washington, sits an elegantly-restored Neo-Classical revival building formerly used as a convent. This bed and breakfast has ten rooms, with traditional furnishings, leaded glass, private baths, TVs, phones, some rooms have water views, fireplaces, and spa tubs. Breakfast is

included and it is only a few blocks to the shops and restaurants of downtown and the banks of the Columbia River.

> 636 Fourteenth St., Astoria, OR 97103
> 800-487-0224
> www.rosebriar.net
> $–$$$

Rockaway Beach
~The Inn On Manhattan Beach
Near Cannon Beach, this little white inn has ten studios, each one- and two- bedroom suites on the oceanfront, with lovely views and a nautical décor. Rooms include kitchens, fireplaces, and spa tubs, and breakfast is available.

> 105 N.W. 23 Ave., Rockaway Beach, OR 97131
> 800-368-6499
> www.river-inn.com
> $–$$$

Gleneden Beach
~Salishan Lodge
Salishan Lodge, on the central coast is a Westin hotel, but it is one of those large hotels that also enables you to feel alone and serene. There are about 200 units tucked into hills and woods, with ocean views, and rooms with fireplaces and balconies. All the amenities of a large resort, such as pool, tennis courts, golf, restaurants, lounge, and fitness center beckon the traveler, but there is also a library and art gallery to relax in for serenity.

> 7760 Hwy. 101 N., Gleneden Beach, OR 97388
> 800-452-2300, 503-764-2371 (Canada and local)
> www.salishan.com
> $$–$$$$$

Yachats
~Overleaf Lodge
Located in one of the quaintest, most scenic towns along the Oregon coast, this 39-room inn, built on top of a bluff, boasts spectacular views from every room. Suites have fireplaces, whirlpool tubs, and balconies. Rooms are more luxurious than most along the coast and the views are divine.

280 Overleaf Lodge Ln., Yachats, OR 97498
800-338-0507
www.overleaflodge.com
$$$–$$$$$

~The See Vue Motel

Don't let the name "motel" fool you at this spectacular bluff-side place. Once you walk into the rooms, the views make you forget that the outside looks like a motel. The two best rooms at this ten-room, gay-friendly inn are the "Princess and the Pea" room or the two-story "Captain's Room."

95590 Hwy. 101, S., Yachats, OR 97498
541-547-3227
www.seevue.com
$–$$

Port Orford
~The Castaway-by-the-Sea Motel

This 13-unit motel is located on a bluff overlooking one of the south coast's most beautiful beaches, with some kitchenettes, glassed-in decks with fabulous views even in the fog, private bathrooms, and comfortable furnishings. Its views and moderate prices make this an ideal spot for creative folks on a budget.

545 5th St., Port Orford, OR 97465
541-332-4502
www.castawaybythesea.com
$–$$

Gold Beach
~Tu Tu' Tun Lodge

Actually seven miles inland on the Rogue River, this elegant lodge has sixteen beautifully decorated rooms, featuring warm earth tones and lots of natural wood; most have king beds, and all have floor-to-ceiling glass windows and views of the river, wood-burning fireplaces, luxurious bathrooms, data ports and business services are available. Suites have kitchens. There is a pool, outdoor spas, and river activities. A hearty breakfast, as well as afternoon snacks and dinner, is available for an additional charge.

96550 N. Bank Rogue, Gold Beach, OR 97444
800-864-6357
www.tututun.com
$$$–$$$$$

Brookings
~Best Western Beachfront Inn
This is a chain motel but it enjoys a fabulous location, on the south coast at the border of Oregon and California with 102 rooms with private balconies overlooking the ocean and bay. It is just steps away from the beach. All rooms have refrigerators, coffee, microwaves, private bathrooms, TV, and phones. Some have kitchenettes and some suites have ocean-view whirlpool tubs. Bring groceries and work on the balcony.

16008 Boat Basin Rd., Harbor, OR 97415
800-468-4081
www.Bestwestern.com/brookings
$$

CALIFORNIA

California

California gets its own chapter. There are thousands of wonderful places to stay in this state, ranging from hostel rooms in a lighthouse to deluxe, luxurious hotels. There are also thousands of writers and artists in California.

From the Oregon Border
Heading South Along the Coast

Crescent City
~Anchor Beach Inn

This is basically a motel with two stories but the views from the balconies overlooking the beach and ocean are wonderful, and it is one of the newest motels in Crescent City, with data ports and second phone lines in the rooms for computers, coffee, available refrigerators and microwaves, guest laundry, some in-room spa tubs and a free continental breakfast. There is an outdoor spa and small pets are allowed.

> 880 Hwy. 101 South, Crescent City, CA 95531
> 800-837-4116
> www.anchorbeachinn.com
> $–$$

Eureka
~Carter House

This is a 32-room restored Victorian mansion in downtown Eureka. Eureka has seeminly hundreds of Victorian buildings, shops, and restaurants. The Carter house also offers suites and cottages or you can rent an entire house with its own kitchen. All rooms have luxurious amenities. Business services, data ports, TV, phone, tea and wine, and a full breakfast are included. The restaurant at the inn has a world-class wine cellar and an excellent chef.

> 301 L St., Eureka, CA 95501
> 800-404-1390

www.carterhouse.com
$$$–$$$$$

Ferndale
~Gingerbread Mansion Inn
This charming, Victorian village south of Eureka, where the movie *Outbreak* was filmed, has several wonderful Victorian bed and breakfasts and this one is perhaps the most well known. A couple of recent large earthquakes have damaged some of the town's historic buildings, but there are many shops and restaurants to visit. The inn has eleven rooms, with private baths, some large with bay windows, some with fireplaces and clawfoot tubs, and all with period antiques. Beautiful English gardens have sitting areas, and a full breakfast and afternoon tea is included.

400 Berding St., Ferndale, CA 95536
800-952-4136
www.gingerbread-mansion.com
$$$–$$$$$

~Victorian Inn
This historic hotel dates back to 1890 during the timber boom era of northern California. The two-story hotel has a restaurant and 12 spacious rooms with private baths, antique furnishings, chandeliers, and high ceilings. A full breakfast is served near the rooms upstairs, and there are fabulous architectural details throughout the building.

400 Ocean Ave., Ferndale, CA 95536
888-589-1808
www.a-victorian-inn.com
$–$$$

Garberville
~Humboldt House Inn (Best Western)
This is an exceptionally pleasant motel, with king and queen rooms with balconies over looking the heated pool and spa and mountains around, but located right in the middle of Garberville's downtown, with its many shops and restaurants. Rooms are air conditioned, have cable TV, data ports, refrigerators, and some have kitchenettes.

701 Redwood Dr., Garberville, CA 95542
862-7756, 707-923-2771
www.bestwestern.com/humboldthouseinn
$–$$

The Victorian Inn, Ferndale, CA. Over one-hundred years old, this charming inn is just one of many Victorian-design buildings in this town that has seen numerous large earthquakes, yet have managed to survive intact. Courtesy of Andrea Brown

~Benbow Inn

This national historic landmark Tudor-styled building is right on the Eel River, with 55 rooms and some suites. There is an elegant dining room in the inn with a terrace overlooking the river and gardens in the back. Sherry is complimentary in each room, and some rooms have spa tubs. There is no elevator in this three-story building, but there are business services available and TV with VCR. The hotel is closed from January through April 7th. Highway 101 is visible from hotel.

445 Lake Benbow Dr., Garberville, CA 95542
707-923-2124 or 800-355-3301, Fax: 707-923-2897
www.benbowinn.com
$$–$$$

Mendocino Coast from Fort Bragg
South on Highway One

Fort Bragg
~Grey Whale Inn

Built in 1915, this historic building is styled in the classic revival style, with high ceilings, large hallways, and plenty of room to stroll. There are fourteen rooms, some with ocean views, decks, and fireplaces but all have private baths, microwaves, refrigerators, coffee, TV, VCR's, local art, and local quilts, and an old-fashioned elegance, though on a foggy day it can feel dark. It is an easy walk to restaurants and shops. A full breakfast is included.

> 615 N. Main St., Fort Bragg, CA 95437
> 800-382-7244
> www.greywhaleinn.com
> **$$–$$$$**

~Beachcomber on the Beach Hotel

There are 72 rooms at this motel, but what makes it special are the rooms that open up right onto the beach with fabulous views of the ocean. Otherwise, these are pretty standard motel rooms, with TV and private baths.

> 1111 N. Main St., Fort Bragg, CA 95437
> 707-964-2402
> www.thebeachcombermotel.com
> **$–$$$$$**

Mendocino

This adorable town, perched on cliffs jutting out into the ocean, was made famous by actress Angela Lansbury filming "Murder She Wrote" here, because it looks more like a coastside town in New England than one in California. There are numerous hotels, inns, and bed and breakfasts, and in off-season, during the week, just come up, drive around and pick one that speaks to you. Otherwise, some favorites:

~MacCallum House Inn

This charming Victorian house, with a wrap around deck overlooking gardens and the water is perched on a hill in the middle of this charming town. It was built in 1882. The main inn has a fabulous restaurant with fireplaces and shelves of books lining many of the walls. An expanded continental breakfast is included, but do have dinner here. Besides the rooms in the main building, there are more luxurious rooms in the carriage house, water tower, and greenhouse all on the garden-filled grounds—nineteen rooms altogether. Some rooms have fireplaces, spa tubs or clawfoot tubs, and water views. This place has a fairytale feel about it, with the perfect mix of quaint and luxurious.

MacCallum House, Mendocino, CA.
Two blocks away from bluffs overlooking the Pacific Ocean, this inn is located in the town where Murder She Wrote *was filmed.*
Courtesy of Eileen Gayle

45020 Albion St., Mendocino, CA 95460
800-609-0492
www.maccallumhouse.com
$$–$$$$

~Joshua Grindle Inn

Located high up on a hill overlooking the water, sits this beautiful Victorian farmhouse with ten rooms and a guest house. A large porch encircles the house, with great ocean and garden views. A terrific full gourmet breakfast is included. The rooms are comfortable and charming and some have water views and spa tubs.

44800 Little Lake Rd., Mendocino, CA 95460
800-GRINDLE
www.joshgrin.com
$$–$$$$$

~Agate Cove Inn

This unassuming, yet charming 1860's farmhouse sits high on a bluff overlooking the Pacific Ocean. Ten rooms, all with private baths and beautiful views, offer king or queen beds, fireplaces, sherry in the rooms, TV/VCR/CD players. Some rooms have spa tubs. A full breakfast is served in the farmhouse overlooking the ocean and coastal gardens. It is located at the north edge of town, just a short ride or a ten-minute walk to shops and restaurants.

11201 N. Lansing St., Mendocino, CA 95460
800-5273111
www.agatecove.com
$$–$$$$$

~Sea Rock Bed and Breakfast Inn

Probably the best views of the ocean in town are to be found from the rooms at this bed and breakfast inn with separate cottages as well as some motel-like units. Located at the north end of town (right next to the Agate Cove Inn mentioned above). There are fourteen rooms and many have private decks and fireplaces; all have private baths and entrances, TV/VCR, telephones, feather beds, and some have spa tubs. Breakfast is an expanded continental and served in the main building or deck overlooking cliffs and surf. There is a sitting area across the street where one can enjoy sunsets. This is a wonderful place to hole up, find inspiration, and the only problem is that you'll never want to check out and leave.

11101 Lansing St., Mendocino, CA 95460
800-906-0926
www.searock.com
$$$–$$$$$

~Stanford Inn By the Sea

High up on a meadow overlooking the ocean, a short distance away, this two-story rustic, yet elegant inn has 33 rooms on expansive grounds with gardens, llamas, an indoor pool, sauna and spa, fireplaces, and sofas in rooms that are decorated with antiques, a TV/VCR, and a full breakfast is included. There is also a restaurant on the premises, as the inn is outside of town on the south side, so you can stay put for an evening here, without driving anywhere else and be utterly content. Massages, kayaks, and boats are available.

P.O. Box 487, 44850 Comptche-Ukiah Rd., Mendocino, CA 95460
800-331-8884
www.stanfordinn.com
$$$$–$$$$$

Little River

~Little River Inn

Just south of Mendocino, on Highway One, sits this beautiful, old inn, built in 1853, with its own golf course and restaurant and bar located on over 200 acres of fabulous hillside overlooking the Pacific. Part of it is a two-story motel with balconies, part of it has new buildings with elegant suites, but my favorite room is in the old inn itself, above the restaurant, with a spectacular ocean view from a small couch in front of the large window in the room. All rooms have private baths with the inn's own soaps and the décor ranges from nice motel to elegant and luxurious new suite rooms, with kitchenettes, fireplaces, and spa tubs.

> P.O. Box B, Little River, CA 95456
> 888-INN-LOVE
> www.Littleriverinn.com.
> $$$–$$$$$

Little River Inn, Little River, CA. Just two miles south of the charming village of Mendocino, this ocean-view inn also has spa facilities available, as well as a golf course on the grounds. Courtesy of Little River Inn

Albion

~Albion River Inn

Just six miles south of Mendocino, on top of a cliff, this inn has twenty lovely rooms, some with amazing ocean views, private entrances, decks, private baths, and spa tubs. There is a full breakfast and wine, coffee and tea are included, as well as an excellent restaurant on the premises. Since there are no distracting shops nearby, this is a serene and inspiring spot for writing.

3790 Hwy. One North, Albion, CA 95410
800-479-7944
www.albionriverinn.com
$$$$–$$$$$

CREATIVE SELF LOOSED

Every writer needs to get away, at least once a year, in order to explore his or her creative options. For me, the ideal place is the Little River Inn, just outside Mendocino, California, where I spend several days in either late December or early January. I always get the same room, which is upstairs in the original building, overlooking both gardens and ocean. I bring with me all the writing projects I want to re-visit, along with journals from previous years and specially-chosen reading materials. Specifically, I bring one new writing tablet, magazines that cover my favorite inspirations—gardening, architecture, art, poetry, and spirituality—and my two favorite authors' works.

There are no distractions and my creative self is turned loose like a playful child. By the time I leave, much has been accomplished: completed projects, new writing, revisions, and most important, a new vision of myself as a writer.

—*Nancy Ellis, literary agent (Nancy Ellis Literary Agency)*

Elk

~*Elk Cove Inn*

This ocean-front mansion, built in 1883, sits on top of a cliff, with stunning views of the rocks below and the ocean. There are fourteen rooms; some are small and a bit dark, so make sure you get one with an ocean view. There are ocean-front spa suites and all rooms have antiques, private baths, robes, coffee, and bedtime port and chocolates. There is private beach access, outdoor hot tub, gardens and a full breakfast is served. A common room downstairs has a TV/VCR, books and games, a full bar and amazing views.

6300 S. Hwy. One, Elk, CA 95432
800-275-2967
www.elkcoveinn.com
$$$–$$$$$

~Greenwood Pier Inn

Truly one of the loveliest places to stay on the north coast, this inn offers of many different types of lodging including separate cottages with private entrances, some two-story, some attached, and two-story one room in the main building that has an upstairs attic and comfy chairs in which to sit and work , while gazing at the ocean and rock caves below. Many of the rooms have spectacular views from cliff-side decks, with sitting areas, fireplaces, and different kinds of décor in different types of rooms. All are done with an artistic eye, all have private baths, and there is an outdoor spa on a cliff, immaculate gardens of flowers, vegetables and herbs that are used by the restaurant on the premises, and a large, continental breakfast is included and brought to your room. There is also a country store and garden shop on the grounds.

> 5928 S. Hwy. One, Box 336, Elk, CA 95432
> 707-877-9997
> www.Greenwoodpierinn.com
> $$–$$$$

~Griffin House at Greenwood Cove

The main house was built in 1890 and now contains a restaurant/pub, but the seven cottages all have private entrances, private baths, and wood-burning stoves. If you stay here, ask for one of the oceanfront cottages with decks above the water. They have comfortable sitting areas for working and breath-taking views. A full breakfast is included and delivered to your room.

> 5910 S. Hwy. One, Box 172, Elk, CA 95432
> 707-877-3422
> www.griffin.com
> $$–$$$

Gualala

Gualala (pronounced Wa-la-la) is a small oceanfront town, with wonderful restaurants, quaint shops and galleries, and plenty of whales watching much of the year. There are parks on the river and ocean beaches, public golf course on the ocean, and views from everywhere.

~St. Orres Inn

Located just two miles north of Gualala, this unusual, Russian style, wooden building has beautiful stained glass throughout. Rvooms upstairs in the main building are small but cozy with balconies and ocean views, but there are also cottages on the grounds. The inn boasts a four-star restaurant.

> 36601 S. Hwy. One, Gualala, CA 95445
> 707-884-3303
> $$–$$$$

~Serenisea

This is a great place for longer stays with separate cottages on the west side of Highway One, atop the cliffs in a shady cluster of trees. All cottages are fully equipped with kitchens, fireplaces, tiled baths, living rooms, a comfortable place to work, and many have fabulous ocean views. There are also vacation homes available to rent for longer stays. Cottages and homes, are fully equipped with supplies. There is a bluff-edge spa outdoors and pets are allowed.

> 36100 Hwy. One South, Gualala, CA 95445
> 707-884-3836
> 800-331-3836
> www.serenisea.com
> $$–$$$$

~Old Milano Hotel

Situated at an amazing location on a bluff above the Pacific Ocean, this hotel has some cottage rooms available after a fire destroyed the old, historic inn that used to be here. It is still a wonderful place to stay and some of the available rooms have incredible ocean views, and all are luxurious in feel.

> 38300 Hwy. One, Gualala, CA 95445
> 707-884-3256
> $$$–$$$$

~Seacliff

This two-story lodge is aptly named, as it is high above the Gualala River, and the beaches of Gualala, and for an ocean-front inn, it probably offers one of the best deals on the entire coast of California. The rooms all face the ocean and have large picture windows, all have fireplaces, private decks, spa tubs under a window, refrigerators (filled with a complimentary bottle of champagne on arrival), TV, and binoculars to whale watch. Next door, there are shops and a wonderful restaurant, Top of the Cliff, with ocean views.

> 39140 S. Hwy. One, Gualala, CA 95445
> 800-400-5053, 707-884-1213
> www.seacliffmotel.com
> **$$–$$$$**

~Sea Ranch Lodge

Just south of the town of Gualala, and over the bridge and Gualala River on the border of Mendocino and Sonoma counties, lies the unique community of Sea Ranch with hundreds of architecturally beautiful homes, many of which are available for rentals—some for one night and some for weekly or monthly rates. Lodge rooms have fireplaces and great views.

> 60 Sea Walk Dr., P.O. Box 44, Sea Ranch, Ca 95497
> 707-785-2371
> **$$$–$$$$**

Boonville
~Boonville Hotel

Between Highway One in Mendocino and Highway 101, Highway 128 goes right through Boonville, and even if you don't stay here, do take the time to stop, and have a look at this beautifully restored, historic hotel with magnificent gardens and gazebos in the back. The grounds are something of an oasis and one can easily spend hours sitting in the chairs scattered throughout the gardens, simply to gaze off into another world of every kind of plant, flower and tree. The inn is furnished in Early American style with antiques, fresh flowers, down comforters, and some rooms have garden views. Some of the rooms are small but all are cozy. Breakfast is included and people come from all over the state to dine in the restaurant downstairs.

> Box 326, Boonville, CA 95415
> 707-895-2210
> www.boonville.com
> **$–$$$**

Bodega Bay

~Inn at the Tides

Most famous for Alfred Hitchcock having filmed *The Birds* here, this is a quiet, fishing harbor town, with a lot of fog. It is also a peaceful, low-key spot for creative types, and this 86-room, two-story inn, on six acres of hillside overlooking the water, has spacious and luxurious rooms with private baths, fireplaces, some patios, sitting areas, and an indoor/outdoor pool sauna and spa, as well as a restaurant on the premises. Continental breakfast is included.

> 800 Coast Hwy., Bodgea Bay, CA 94923
> 800-541-7788
> www.innatthetides.com
> $$$–$$$$$

~Bodega Bay Lodge & Spa *

Perched on a hill with beautiful sand dunes and native grasses and overlooking the water, this is an elegant 84-room motel with large rooms, some with lofts, private baths, fireplaces, TV/HBO, and balconies overlooking the bay and ocean. The amenities are luxurious, and there are business services available, as well as a pool, spa and sauna, ocean-view fitness center, a restaurant and a complimentary wine hour. Suites and two-bedroom quarters are enormous.

> 103 Coast Hwy. 1, Bodega Bay, CA 94923
> 800-368-2468
> www.woodsidehotels.com
> $$$$–$$$$$

Guerneville

~Applewood Inn, The Estate

Located along the Russian River in Sonoma County, this elegantly-appointed mansion in Mission revival-style architecture has ten suites that include private bath, phones, data ports, cable TV, fresh flowers, queen beds, evening turn-down service with chocolates, and a complimentary full breakfast. Furnishings are individualized in soft pastel colors with original art and antiques and the rooms are spacious and soothing. The common rooms, including a library, are inviting, with hardwood floors, European and American art, cozy sitting areas, and elegant details throughout, with woods and gardens surrounding the hotel. There is a pool, spa, and no children are allowed which provides a serene and relaxing environment.

13555 Hwy. 116, Guerneville, CA 95446
707-869-9093, 800-555-8509
www.applewoodinn.com
$$$$–$$$$$

The Estate, Guerneville, CA. Many award-winning Sonoma county wineries are within a few minutes drive of this luxurious inn. Courtesy of Darryl Notter

Occidental
~Inn at Occidental

This fourteen-room inn has won many awards as one of the top inns in the West. Its folk art, antiques, charm and attention to detail make it a favorite among bed and breakfast afficionados. Rooms have down comforters on featherbeds, private baths, decks, phones, DSL and business services, fireplaces, and some rooms and suites have sitting areas, and spa tubs. A full, hearty breakfast as well as afternoon hors d'oeuvres are included. The large veranda is covered with comfortable wicker furniture and is a great place to read and write.

> 3657 Church St., Box 857, Occidental, CA 95465
> 800-522-6324
> www.innatoccidental.com
> $$$$–$$$$$

Olema
~Olema Inn

Located by the Point Reyes National Seashore area in Marin County, this restored old inn is quiet, charming, and away-from-it-all, yet reasonably close to San Francisco. Originally built in 1876, the six rooms all have private baths, charming details, and there are pretty gardens and a patio, and rates include an expanded breakfast. The inn's restaurant is also wonderful.

> 10000 Sir Francis Drake Blvd., Olema, CA 94950
> 800-532-9252
> www.theolemainn.com
> $$–$$$$$

Inverness
~Blackthorne Inn

This unusual bed and breakfast was built in 1975, from redwood that was cut and milled on the premises, and the five guest rooms are all unique, such as the "Eagle's Nest" up in a tower. All have private baths and elegant amenities. A full breakfast is included and is served weather-permitting on the huge redwood deck, overlooking the San Andreas Fault near the Point Reyes National Seashore.

266 Vallejo Ave., Inverness Park, CA 94937
415-663-8621
www.blackthorneinn.com
$$$$–$$$$$

Napa and Sonoma Counties

The wine country of Northern California is beautiful and some areas are certainly conducive to hiding away to reflect, write, or create art. However, due to the high cost of many places in this area, and all the distractions of the charming towns, the numerous wineries, expensive restaurants, and many activities, it is not really a recommended location for the purposes of this book, so I have included only a few special places:

Healdsburg
~Madrona Manor

A Victorian mansion on eight magnificently landscaped acres, this inn and restaurant was built in 1881. There are rooms upstairs in the original building boasting high ceilings and period pieces, as well as rooms in the carriage house. All seventeen rooms and five suites are decorated with lavish antiques, have air conditioning, private baths, and most have fireplaces, king and queen beds but no TVs. A wraparound veranda, the gardens and a heated pool are perfect places to sit and reflect. The renowned restaurant serves dinners in small, intimate, antique-laden rooms replete with candlelight

1001 Westside Rd., Healdsburg, CA , 95448
707-433-4231, 800-258-4003
www.madronamanor.com
$$$$–$$$$$

~Camellia Inn

Originally built in 1869, this inn has nine individually decorated rooms with hardwood floors, chandeliers, oriental rugs, antiques, some with private entrances, fireplaces, and spa tubs or stained glass, and most with private baths. There is a pool in the back and camellia plants surrounding the house and lawn. A breakfast is included and afternoon wine is served in the double parlors downstairs.

211 N. St., Healdsburg, CA 95448
707-433-8182, 800-727-8182
www.camelliainn.com
$–$$$

~Healdsburg Inn on the Plaza

Located right on the Healdsburg town square, above an art gallery and gift shop, this Victorian inn has nine unique and elegantly appointed rooms with private baths, lots of antiques and local artists' works, clawfoot tubs and other luxurious amenities. There is a garden-solarium room where both breakfast—included in the price of the room—and freshly baked cookies are served. For some people, the shops, wineries and cafes on the square may be too much of a distraction.

110 Matheson St., Healdsburg, CA 95448
707-433-6991
www.healdsburginn.com
$$$–$$$$$

~Grape Leaf Inn

This beautifully restored 1900 Queen Anne Victorian home has seven rooms with private baths, including spa tubs, air conditioning, antique furnishings, in a quiet, residential part of town. Included are a full breakfast, as well as afternoon cheese and local wines. This is one of the most reasonable inns in the area with a very homey feeling.

539 Johnson St., Healdsburg, CA 95448
707-433-8140
www.grapeleafinn.com
$$–$$$$

Santa Rosa

~Vintners Inn

This is an European-style, two story hotel, with 44 large rooms with beamed ceilings, antique French pine furnishings, TV, data ports, refrigerators, large private bathrooms with brass detailing, and some have vineyard views as the inn is surrounded by over 40 acres of vineyards. The grounds are lovely with fountains, gardens, a pool, spa, library and large continental breakfast is included. An excellent restaurant is located on the premises.

Camellia Inn, Healdsburg, CA. True to its name, camellia bushes cover the landscape of this quaint inn, even around the pool. Courtesy of Diana Bradley

4350 Barnes Rd., Santa Rosa, CA 95403
800-421-2584
www.vintnersinn.com
$$$–$$$$

Sonoma

~Victorian Garden Inn

On an acre with lovely gardens, yet just two blocks from the town square and wineries, this 1870 farmhouse has four rooms decorated with antiques with views of the pool, hot tub, and gardens. An expanded continental breakfast is served in the dining room, garden, or your own room.

316 E. Napa St., Sonoma, CA 95476
800-543-5339
www.victoriangardeninn.com
$$–$$$$

Kenwood

~Kenwood Inn & Spa

A few minutes north of the town of Sonoma, this sophisticated Mediterranean-style villa is located in the middle of vineyards, and all the elegant rooms have private baths, fireplaces, down comforters, wines and chocolates, and a full breakfast is served. There is a pool, a spa and beautifully-landscaped gardens among the vineyards.

10400 Sonoma Hwy., Kenwood, CA 95452
707-833-1293, 800-353-6966
www.kenwoodinn.com
$$$–$$$$$

Glen Ellen

~Gaige House Inn

This award-winning bed and breakfast has fifteen rooms and suites and is located in the quiet and lovely literary town of Glen Ellen, temporary home of author Jack London. Sophisticated and elegant surroundings that are influenced by Asian and West Indian décor, pretty gardens and a short walk to shops and restaurants make this a romantic and serene spot. The rooms have TV, air conditioning, orchids, phones, high-end furnishings in earthy tones, and some have fireplaces, decks, and spa tubs. On a nearby creek, there is a heated pool, spa, hammock, and picnic tables. Included at this gay-friendly inn are a fabulous breakfast, snacks, and evening wine and appetizers.

13540 Arnold Dr., Glen Ellen, CA 95442
800-935-0237
www.gaige.com
$$$–$$$$$

Napa

~The Beazley House Inn

Located in a residential neighborhood of charming, old houses within historic downtown Napa sits the beautiful Beazley mansion. The eleven elegant rooms have private baths, fireplaces, spa tubs, and antique furnishings. Low fat gourmet breakfasts are included.

1910 First St., Napa, CA 94559
800-559-1649
www.beazleyhouse.com
$$$–$$$$$

St. Helena

~Harvest Inn

The English Tudor-style hotel has 54 elegant rooms with sitting areas, private baths, fireplaces, wet bars, refrigerators, vanities, TV, air conditioning, telephones and all the luxurious amenities of a fine hotel. There are two pools and spas, spacious meeting rooms, an oak-paneled great room, gardens, and the inn overlooks fourteen acres of vineyards. A full breakfast is included amid this story-book atmosphere.

One Main St., St. Helena, CA 94574
800-950-8466
www.harvestinn.com
$$–$$$$$

~The Wine Country Inn

Located on a hill overlooking vineyards, this 21-room country inn is charming and quiet, as it is siturated on a small road outside of St. Helena.

HOME AWAY FROM HOME

Stealing away to finish your creative work, while a reprieve from everyday tasks and distractions, still requires organization and some light housekeeping. Financial guru Suze Orman and I made several week-long trips to the Sonoma wine country to finish our first book, *You've Earned It, Don't Lose It*. The two-room cottage we rented (with kitchen) was planted in the middle of a vineyard. We purposely opted for complete seclusion with no outside diversions, including housekeeping staff which, we thought, would have been yet another distraction.

We arrived, provisions in hand, set up our laptops and printers, and created a daily plan.

The routine went something like this: After a breakfast of oatmeal to sustain us, we washed the dishes and began writing. We broke for lunch (we had made a large pot of homemade soup the first day) and washed the dishes, broke for an afternoon walk and discussion, broke for dinner (more soup until it ran out) and washed those dishes, broke for the evening news (we carted up a mini TV on our second and subsequent trips) and calls to home, and then worked until midnight.

While we would all like to think that our creativity is spontaneous, the most experienced among us knows that it requires planning. Having a home away from home at first seemed like extra work, but it succeeded because we had a routine!

—*Linda Mead, author of* You've Earned It, Don't Lose It *with Suze Orman and* Walking With Giants, *and literary agent with LitWest Group LLC*

The cozy rooms have private baths, quilts, pine antiques, and fireplaces. Balconies overlook the surrounding hills. There are also three suites. A full breakfast and afternoon wine and appetizers are included.

> 1152 Lodi Ln., St. Helena, CA 94574
> 888-465-4608
> www.winecountryinn.com.
> $$$–$$$$$

Yountville

Just nine miles north of the city of Napa is one of the prettiest little towns in all of California—Yountville.

~Burgundy House Inn

The Burgundy House country inn is a French country stone building built in the 1870's from local stone and rock. The walls are almost two feet thick, there are wooden beams, rustic masonry, and antique country furniture throughout. The five rooms have private baths, fresh flowers, local complimentary wine, and a full breakfast is served in the garden or "distillery" room.

> 6711 Washington St., Yountville, CA 94599
> 707-944-0889
> www.burgundyhouse.com
> $$–$$$

~Napa Valley Railway Inn

This is one of the more unusual places to stay in California, and the ten rooms here are actual turn-of-the century train cars, complete with cabooses, elegantly restored with antique furnishings, comfy queen brass beds, skylights and bay windows, plush chairs, private baths, and entrances off a promenade deck. A few steps away are shops and restaurants.

> 6503 Washington St., Yountville, CA 94599
> 707-944-2000
> $–$$$

Clear Lake

Lakeport

~Skylark Shores Motel Resort

This 45-unit motel is set on attractive, spacious grounds overlooking scenic Clear Lake. Rooms are standard motel fare but include patios and balconies and there is a pool with a boating dock.

> 1120 N. Main St., Lakeport, CA 95453
> 707-263-6151
> $-$$

CONFESSIONS OF A BINGE WRITER

Conventional wisdom dictates that a dedicated writer must write every day, at the same time each day. But as a working mom in a troubled marriage, there was no way my novel was ever going to get written if I tried to follow that rule. Instead of beating myself up about this, I decided to define myself as a "binge writer." I found a distraction-free motel in Lake County, California, over three hours' drive from my San Francisco home, where I could rent a private cabin at reasonable off-season rates. I went there whenever I could—even if it was just for a couple of days—and wrote nonstop. Then I'd come home and let the writing sit for a while, or work on edits and revisions.

The bonus was that I ended up setting my story in Lake County, and when my book was finally finished and published, I made sure the folks up there knew it. I donated a percentage of my book advance to the Lake County Library's Family Literacy Program, and set up a reading at a small local bookstore. I still get letters from people who found my book, read it, and are looking for the fictional honky-tonk bar in which I set a lot of the action!

So my advice is this: If the rules don't work for you, make up new ones. Always try to find a local or personal angle when it is time to promote your book, and if you're writing fiction, it's okay to make stuff up.

Oh, and if you are looking for a writer's hideaway a bit off the beaten path in Northern California, try the Skylark Shores Motel in Lakeport, California. Tell 'em Sarah Jean Pixlie sent you.

—Kathi Kamen Goldmark, author of And My Shoes Keep Walking Back To You, *former publicist at HarperCollins, and member of the Rock Bottom Remainders literary band.*

Lake Tahoe

Lake Tahoe is a gorgeous lake deep in the Sierra-Nevada Mountains that border California and Nevada.

Tahoe Vista

~Shore House at Lake Tahoe

This is a rustic waterfront inn with nine rooms with private baths and one separate cottage. Rooms have pine walls and log furniture, down comforters, featherbeds, fireplaces, and many have spectacular lake views. There is a pier, beach, decks, outdoor spa, and gardens on the grounds and a full breakfast, wine and appetizers, and baked treats are included.

> 7170 N. Lake Blvd., Tahoe Vista, CA 96148
> 800-207-5160
> www.shorehouselaketahoe.com
> $$$–$$$$$

South Lake Tahoe
~The Chateau Inn & Suites
This inn has rooms, spa, and fireplace suites, some with lake or mountain views, private beach access, outdoor spa, microwaves and refrigerators and interior hallways with covered parking for cars. A complimentary continental breakfast is included and ski packages are available. If you feel the need for a gambling break, it is only two blocks to casinos.

> 965 Park Ave., South Lake Tahoe, CA 96150
> 800-455-6060
> www.chateausuites.com
> $–$$$$

Tahoe City
~Chaney House
This historic lakefront stone house has four rooms, surrounded by woods overlooking the west side of the lake. Built in the 1920s by Italian stone masons, the architecture is magnificent, with a huge stone fireplace and cathedral ceiling. Rooms have private baths and are quite comfortable. A full breakfast is included and served on the patio overlooking the lake, pier, and private beach.

> 4725 W. Lake Blvd., Tahoe City, CA 96145
> 530-525-7333
> www.chaneyhouse.com
> $$$–$$$$

Squaw Valley
~Valley Lodge
Located high up in the mountains of the Olympics locale, Squaw Valley, this all-suite condominium hotel has kitchens, lots of space, views of moun-

tains, a pool, indoor spas, a health club, and wonderful hiking trails where you can clear your head.

> 201 Squaw Peak Rd., Olympic Valley, CA 96146
> 800-765-3145
> www.squawvalleylodge.com
> $$–$$$$$

Gold Rush Country

Only a few hours drive from the Bay area and close to Sacramento, there are numerous charming Gold Rush towns along Highway 49. A few of our favorites are:

Murphys
~Murphys Historic Hotel and Lodge

A registered historic Landmark Hotel originally built in 1856, the 29 rooms include historic rooms in the original inn (with shared baths) or more modern motel-like rooms next door (stay in the old inn). There are private baths, TV, phones (in the motel wing), and a saloon and restaurant. The lodge is located in the middle of a quaint town with shops, wineries and restaurants. President Grant once stayed here, and the room named for him is especially wonderful.

> 457 Main St., Murphys, CA 95247
> 800-532-7684
> $–$$$

Angels Camp
~Angel's Hacienda (formerly The Redbud Inn)

This is an inn in an historic town, with eight spacious suites, beautifully decorated with private baths, wood stoves or fireplaces, balconies with views, spa tubs, and bay windows. Also, a suite with two rooms is available and a full, hearty breakfast is included, as well as afternoon wine and snacks. There are spa facilities.

> 4871 Hunt Rd., Angels Camp, CA 95222
> 209-728-8533, 800-827-8533

www.redbudinn.com
$$–$$$$$

~Cooper House Bed & Breakfast

Built in 1911, this is a charming house, with gardens and a fabulous great room with fireplace and antiques. The three rooms have private baths, air conditioning, sitting areas, and an expanded continental breakfast and afternoon drinks and snacks are included.

1184 Church St., Angels Camp, CA 95222
209-736-2145
$$

Sonora

~Bradford Place Inn and Gardens

This charming 1889 Victorian inn, surrounded by a white picket fence, has four rooms containing antiques, phones, data port, digital answering machines, TV/VCR, coffee, air conditioning and some with fireplaces, refrigerators and microwaves. The baths are attached. A full breakfast and afternoon treats are included and served in the lovely garden.

56 W. Bradford St., Sonora, CA 95370
800-209-2315
www.bradfordplaceinn.com
$–$$$

Columbia

~City Hotel and Fallon Hotel

This hotel is located in the unique state historical park of Columbia, which is the only totally preserved Gold-Rush town in the state. The historic part of the town established in 1857, feels and looks exactly like it did in the 1800s, no cars allowed, and while there are some shops and restaurants, there are mostly museums and historically themed businesses. The City Hotel is in the middle of town, has ten rooms, some with large balconies, and all with magnificent antique furnishings. There are toilets in the rooms, although a shared shower room is in the main hallway. There are central heating and cooling systems, but otherwise guests are transported back to the Gold-Rush era, meaning no TVs. Staff are dressed in period costumes. The Fallon Hotel, on the edge of town, has fourteen rooms and was renovated in 1986. It still retains the same charm as it did in the 1860s but has private baths. The restaurant in the City Hotel is a well-known gourmet restaurant with period décor. This is a perfect place to write historical fiction.

P.O. Box 1870, Main St., Columbia, CA 95310
209-532-1479
$$

Amador City
~Mine House Inn
This is a beautiful, historic inn with two buildings, eight rooms, and five luxury suites, with fireplaces and large spa tubs. Breakfast is included and antique furnishings abound.

Box 245, Amador City, CA 95601
800-646-3473
www.minehouseinn.com
$$–$$$$$

Sutter Creek
~Sutter Creek Inn
A beautiful and peaceful bed and breakfast, with eighteen unusual rooms, including a library room—perfect for writers—rooms with swinging beds which can be stabilized for sleeping, and cozy fireplace rooms. Some rooms, all containing private baths and air conditioning, are in the main building where a big breakfast is served in the dining room, and others are scattered throughout the garden-filled grounds, with secret nooks and hammocks. Shops and restaurants are just steps away in quaint Sutter Creek.

75 Main St., Sutter Creek, CA 95685
209-267-5606
www.suttercreekinn.com
$–$$$$

~Foxes in Sutter Creek
Winner of many awards, this charming inn has seven rooms all elegantly appointed with antique furnishings emphasizing the fox theme through-

out, private baths, fireplaces, TV/VCR and air conditioning. A full breakfast, served on sterling silver, either in the garden or in your room, is included. Sit on the front porch and watch the main street action.

77 Main St., Sutter Creek, CA 95685
800-987-3344
www.foxesinn.com
$$$–$$$$

Nevada City
~Grandmere's Inn
An elegant mansion listed on National Register of Historic Places, this
inn has six romantic rooms with private baths, large rooms with four-poster
beds, and one suite has a private parlor and soaking tub. The formal gardens
are beautiful and a large breakfast is included.

449 Broad St., Nevada City, CA 95959
530-265-4660
www.nevadacityinns.com
$$–$$$$

Yosemite National Park
~The Redwoods
Located six miles inside the south entrance of the park, The Redwoods
provides approximately 100 houses and cottages, from one-bedroom cabins
to a luxurious five-bedroom home. The cabins are fully equipped with kitchen
supplies, firewood, linens, and everything you need except for your personal
items and work supplies. Comfortably furnished with lots of wood detailing, some cottages have decks and barbecues.

Box 2085, Yosemite National Park, CA 95389
209-375-6666
www.Redwoodsinyosemite.com
$$–$$$$$

~Wawona Hotel
This National Historic Landmark hotel was built in 1879 and truly rep-
resents the grandeur of that time. The 104 rooms are charming and cozy

with all the amenities necessary and the front veranda is a delight. Located at the south entrance of the park for a quieter locale. Across from the hotel is a nine-hole golf course.

> Yosemite National Park, CA 95389
> 559-252-4848
> www.yosemite.nationa-park.com/lodge.htm
> $–$$$

Yosemite Valley
~The Ahwahnee

Even if you don't stay here, this is a Yosemite landmark that must be seen. This elegant, seven-story hotel, with 123 rooms, is magnificent itself, but the woods, mountains, waterfalls and nature around it are just as spectacular. Built in 1927, the granite and concrete exterior were stained to look like redwood. Some rooms are fairly small but others are spacious enough to feel roomy. Some have desks and some don't so ask ahead. All have private baths, phones, comfortable furnishings, and all the necessary aspects of a large hotel There is a bar, a fantastic restaurant, a magnificent lobby with priceless art, rugs, and photos, common areas, and a gift shop.

> Yosemite Valley, CA 95389
> 559-252-4848
> www.yosemite.nationa-park.com/lodge.htm
> $$$$$

San Francisco Bay Area

This is the "City by the Bay" and is characterized by a wonderful mix of art, culture, scenic beauty and great restaurants. San Francisco is not the best city to hideaway in as there are just too many distractions, but, if you one who can still focus on your work while tempted, here are some great spots to visit:

San Francisco
~Petite Auberge and White Swan Inn

Next door to each other in Nob Hill, these "Four Sisters Inns" are elegant and sophisticated, with beautifully-appointed rooms with flowered wallpaper, plush pillows and chairs, data ports, thick comforters, French art and glass, fireplaces, and all the luxurious amenities expected of this fine chain of country inns. All rooms have private baths, and breakfast and afternoon tea and hors d'oeuvres are included.

Petite Auberge
863 Bush St., San Francisco, CA 94108
800-365-3004
$$–$$$$$

White Swan
845 Bush St., San Francisco, CA 94108
800-999-9570
$$$–$$$$$

~The Cartwright Hotel

Located on Union Square, this landmark, European-style hotel has totally renovated its 114 rooms with flowery prints, period furniture, modern, private baths, desks, data ports, honor bar and voice mail. Included in the room price are a continental breakfast buffet, wine reception from 5-6 P.M. each evening, and coffees and teas that are served in the library off the lobby. Rooms and bathrooms are small, but for the location and price, you can't beat it.

524 Sutter St., San Francisco, CA 94102
800-919-9779
www.cartwrighthotel.com
$–$$$$$

The Cartwright Hotel, San Francisco, CA. This "boutique" Victorian hotel is only two blocks from Union Square, the heart of the shopping district of San Francisco, but be sure to get back to the hotel around five o'clock for the wonderful wine and cheese hour. Courtesy of David Spiselman

~The Hotel Majestic

Located in the beautiful Pacific Heights part of the city, this five-story Edwardian-style hotel, built in 1902, has bay windows and lovely décor is a little oasis. The lobby is elegant and there is a sophisticated restaurant off to the side, with a full bar, styled with mahogany and granite. The 57 rooms have French and British antiques, four-poster canopy beds, marble fireplaces, cable TV, data ports, clawfoot tubs, robes, and European amenities. There are classic and luxurious details throughout the hotel and complimentary wine is served in the afternoon.

> 1500 Sutter St., San Francisco, CA 94109
> 800-869-8966
> www.Thehotelmajestic.com
> $$$$–$$$$$

~Sir Francis Drake Hotel

Since 1928, this has been an elegant, landmark San Francisco hotel located at Union Square. There are over 400 fully-appointed guest rooms, but it's the ornate and very red and gold lobby with early American and European antiques, and the location that makes this place so special. There's an exercise room, full business services, gift shops, restaurants, and the other usual hotel amenities.

> 450 Powell St., San Francisco, CA 94102
> 800-227-5480
> www.Sirfrancisdrake.com
> $$–$$$$

~Cathedral Hill Hotel

In the middle of Van Ness Avenue (also Highway 101 local), between Nob Hill and Pacific Heights sits this block-long, 400-room hotel, built in 1960. It has all the amenities of a large hotel, including an outdoor, heated pool, workout room, restaurant, and lounge, and some rooms have balconies with great city views. All rooms have coffee, data ports, modem lines, desks, and private baths, but there is nothing fancy about them, and the prices are quite reasonable.

> 1101 Van Ness Ave., San Francisco, CA 94109
> 866-823-9330

www.Cathedralhillhotel.com
$–$$$$

~Archbishop's Mansion

Built in 1904 for the Archbishop of San Francisco, this magnificent mansion sits among all the famous "Painted Ladies" in the Victorian section of Alamo Square. For a quieter bed and breakfast experience in the city, this place can't be beat, with its fifteen rooms all named for different operas. All rooms and suites have private baths, beautiful antique furnishings, fireplaces, and some have spa tubs and park views. Complimentary breakfast and afternoon wine are served.

1000 Fulton St., San Francisco, CA 94117
800-543-5820
www.archbishopsmansion.com
$$$$–$$$$$

Berkeley
~The Radisson Hotel

Located right at the Berkeley Marina and on the bay, this 375-room hotel is your basic fancy Radisson(now owned by Hilton), but with gardens and bay views that make it a perfect escape without leaving the East Bay area. There is also a boat dock, health club, enclosed pool, spa and sauna, and restaurant and lounge and all business services are available.

200 University Ave., Berkeley, CA 94710
800-333-3333, 510-548-7920
www.ci.Berkeley.ca.us or www.Radisson.com
$$$–$$$$

San Rafael
~Gerstle Park Inn

This 100-year-old estate has twelve beautiful rooms decorated individually with antiques, and includes private baths, spa tubs, parlors, decks, TV/VCR, phones with modems, robes, sherry, and other treats. The inn sits on 1½ acres of fruit trees and redwoods overlooking the city of San Rafael. A full breakfast and wine hour are included.

34 Grove St., San Rafael, CA 94901
800-726-7611
www.gerstleparkinn.com
$$$–$$$$$

Fremont

~Lord Bradley's Inn

Located in the East Bay, next to Mission San Jose, this bed and breakfast built in the 1870s survived the earthquake and fire that destroyed most of the mission years ago. The Victorian's eight rooms, all with private baths, are named after members of the lord's family—Lady Violet, Sir Douglas, and Lady Hannah. Complimentary breakfast and afternoon refreshments are served in the lovely common rooms. Palm trees dot the grounds that lie below Mission Peak.

43344 Mission Blvd., Fremont, CA 94539
510-490-0520
www.lordbradleysinn.com
$$

LUXURY OF CHOICE

One needs quiet time to write—to form undisturbed and focused thoughts, and sometimes it is necessary to have a special place. That place can act as a muse, of sorts—a way to allow the creative juices to flow. Getting away can stimulate one's characters to visit, to raise their voices and show the writer the way they should continue along their journey.

A writer must ask himself, where do I feel the most at peace? Is it the beach? Is it in a forest setting? The mountains? Some writers prefer to be in cafes and write amongst a bustle of activity. The truth is, one can write anywhere if it is necessary to do so. The best writers are driven to write, sometimes against all odds. They must write, and so they do. If one is lucky enough to have the luxury of a choice of where to write, one must listen to his or her inner voice and heart—and then follow.

—*Kimberley Cameron, literary agent with Reece-Halsey Agency*

Menlo Park
~Stanford Park Hotel

Home of Stanford University, Palo Alto is a city filled with wonderful restaurants, shops, and bookstores. And, this is the nicest hotel in the mid-Peninsula. There are 163 rooms and suites that are spacious and filled with amenities such as double vanities with granite make-up mirrors, hardwood headboards, armoires and big desks, robes, Internet access, and some rooms have fireplaces and balconies, or high ceilings and sitting areas. All the details are luxurious and fairly modern, as the hotel was opened in 1984. There is a fitness room, a heated pool, a spa, and a sauna. Driving up to the lobby, you are surrounded by palm trees. Complimentary coffee, wine and cookies are available.

> 100 El Camino Real, Menlo Park, CA 94025
> 650-322-1234
> www.woodsidehotels.com
> $$$$$

South of San Francisco along Coastal Highway One

Pacifica
~Pacifica Beach Resort

Just opened in 2003, this hotel, 15 minutes down Highway One from San Francisco, has 52 rooms and suites, all with fabulous ocean views, private baths, spa tubs, fireplaces, refrigerators, and high-speed Internet access. There is a heated pool and a restaurant. Complimentary coffee in lobby.

> 525 Crespi Dr., Pacifica, CA 94044
> 650-355-9999
> www.pacificabeachresort.com
> $$-$$$

~Pacifica Motor Inn

A few steps away from the ocean at Rockaway Beach sits this unassuming motel with a tiny bit of Victorian architecture, but the views from rooms on the second and third floors are amazing. There are 42 modern rooms, with private baths, refrigerators, microwaves and tables by the windows with cliff and ocean views. This inn is nothing fancy, but it is clean and inexpensive considering the inspiring views. Continental breakfast is included in room price.

200 Rockaway Beach Ave., Pacifica, CA 94044
800-522-3773
www.pacificamotorinn.com
$–$$

GOING TO THE MATTRESSES

While finishing the manuscript for the sequel to *Rain Fall*, a strategic retreat to a hotel (two, actually) made for my most productive burst of writing ever. The advantages of a hotel are just what you would expect: quiet, private, minimum distractions, and room service to boot. There's also a related, less obvious bonus. When a writer "goes to the mattresses," family and friends know that it's do-or-die time and won't confuse an insistence on solitude with rudeness or impending dementia.

Picking the right hotel is easy—as nice as you can afford is probably a good rule of thumb. Regardless of where you stay, though, timing is the key to making the experience worthwhile. First, the retreat should coincide with an impending deadline (nothing like a little pressure to make one take advantage of the other advantages of a hotel). Second, try to be done with the bulk of what I think of as "concept work": the background thinking that lays the foundation for characters and their motivations and for the trajectory of the plot. No sense achieving all that splendid privacy if you are only going to pace the room the whole time trying to figure out what happens next, right?

I holed up at my local Stanford Park Hotel for two nights of intensive writing. On the last night—early morning, actually— I turned out about 6,500 words, the last two of which were "the end." A nice demonstration, I think, of how much a writer can do when the plot path is clear and distractions have been eliminated.

—*Barry Eisler, bestselling author of* Rain Fall *and* Hard Rain, *Putnam (PenguinGroup)*

Montara

~Farallone View Inn

This seaside bed and breakfast, built in 1906, is on the funky side but some of the rooms have incredible ocean views and large decks. Each of the nine rooms in the three-story inn is unique, and so some have stained glass windows, some have steps, but all have private baths with spa tubs and sitting areas. Breakfast is included.

> 1410 Main St., Montara, CA 94037
> 800-350-9777
> $–$$$

~Point Montara Lighthouse AYH-Hostel

This is one of the only places along the California coast where you can find an oceanfront room for under $40 a night. It also has one of the most spectacular views of any place in California, with rugged cliffs and crashing surf below a real lighthouse. There are shared bunk-bed rooms for about $19 a night, and some private rooms with shared bath. A common kitchen, picnic tables, and cool ocean breezes round out the offer. This is a divine spot anytime for writers and artists, but it is especially nice in fall and spring, or in the winter when storms come off the Pacific. Summers can be foggy and cold.

> P.O. Box 737, Montara, CA 94037
> 650-728-7177
> $

Half Moon Bay

~Cypress Inn on Miramar Beach

A true "beach house," this bed and breakfast sits directly above Miramar Beach at the north end of historic and quaint Half Moon Bay. The eighteen rooms with private baths are all comfortably furnished with wicker furniture, TV, fireplace, phone, tiled floors, skylights, and all are decorated in pastel colors and have folk art work. About half of the rooms have spectacular ocean views and balconies, with the pounding surf below. Breakfast and afternoon wine, appetizers and dessert, are complimentary.

> 407 Mirada Rd., Half Moon Bay, CA 94019
> 800-83-BEACH

www.cypressinn.com
$$$$–$$$$$

~Mill Rose Inn

This is a two-story white building that you barely notice because the gardens, flowers, and trees cover most of it. This romantic bed and breakfast feels more like a botanical garden than an inn, although the six rooms are beautiful and cozy. The rooms are all located upstairs, and all have private baths, some have bay windows and window seats, all are beautifully decorated with floral prints and antiques. A full champagne breakfast is included. Located right in town, the inn is steps away from restaurants and shops.

615 Mill St., Half Moon Bay, CA 94019
800-900-7673
www.millroseinn.com
$$$$–$$$$$

Mill Rose Inn, Half Moon Bay, CA. Weddings are popular here, due to the lush and vibrant gardens surrounding the inn on all sides, and great shops and restaurants are located within a two block radius and the beach is just a short walk away. Courtesy of David Spiselman

Pescadero

~Estancia del Mar

On a bluff, overlooking the ocean and the Pigeon Point Lighthouse are five attached cottages, with separate kitchens, living rooms (some with screened porch), private baths and bedrooms. All the necessities are included, plus a VCR with a film library but no TV. Furnishings are comfortable, though a bit worn, and there are tables to work on against the window with breathtaking views. Bring groceries and stay a few days.

> 460 Pigeon Point Rd., Pescadero, CA 94060
> 650-879-1500
> $–$$$

~Old Saw Mill Lodge

This five-room inn is for when you really want to get away from it all as it is down two miles on a private road, at the top of a wooded mountain that is part of the Santa Cruz mountain range, high above the small town of Pescadero. On a clear day, some rooms have an ocean view. There are sixty acres to stroll about, and an indoor pool, spa, and decks in the lodge, where each room is uniquely decorated with printed fabrics, antiques, hard wood floors, rugs, and private baths. There is a homey feeling here and a wonderful breakfast and afternoon refreshments are included. The innkeeper studied at the California Culinary Academy. Bring some food along, as it is a long way to a store or restaurant.

> 700 Ranch Rd. W., Pescadero, CA 94060
> 800-596-6455
> $$–$$$$

~Pigeon Point Lighthouse American Youth Hostel

This hostel is not just for youths and it has some private rooms are available for reasonable rates. Amazing views and outdoor spa, as well as common rooms and a kitchen make this a fabulous hideaway. Book ahead for private rooms.

> 210 Pigeon Point Rd., Pescadero, CA 94060
> 650-879-0633
> $

Davenport
~Davenport Bed and Breakfast Inn
This quiet oceanside inn sits between Half Moon May and Santa Cruz on the east side of Highway One. Some of the twelve rooms have verandas with ocean views, all have private baths and phones, and a continental breakfast is included. Peaceful and serene with few diversions, this is a wonderful hideaway. There is also a restaurant and gift shop on the premises.

One P. O. Box J, Davenport, CA 95017
800-870-1817
www.Swanton.com
$-$$$

Santa Cruz
~Sea & Sand Inn
Perched on a cliff above Monterey Bay and just a few blocks from the Boardwalk, pier, and shops, this inn has fabulous ocean views from the attached cottages. There are basic queen bedrooms, as well as deluxe king bedrooms with spa tubs. Complimentary continental breakfast, afternoon refreshments, and in winter off-season, wine and cheese are served.

201 W. Cliff Dr., Santa Cruz, CA 95060
831-427-3400
www.santacruzmotels.com
$$-$$$$$

Aptos
~Historic Sand Rock Farm Bed & Breakfast Inn
This beautifully restored inn was originally built in the 1880s from winery ruins on ten acres. There are five rooms, all with private, tiled baths, Internet access and comfortable, fluffy beds. A gourmet breakfast is included.

6901 Freedom Blvd. Aptos, CA
831-688-8005
$$-$$$

Capitola-by-the-Sea
~Inn at Depot Bay
There are six rooms and six suites in this beautiful Mediterranean-style inn, all with private baths, robes, flowers, phones, TV/VCR, stereos, feather-

beds, Internet access, fireplaces, coffee, and each room is luxuriously decorated in world themes such as Paris, Kyoto, and Portofino. Many of the rooms have private spas on their own patios that provide a really decadent feel. A full breakfast, afternoon wine, appetizers and desserts are included in the price of the room. It's a short drive to the beach.

> 250 Monterey Ave., Capitola, CA 95010
> 800-572-2632
> www.innatdepothill.com
> $$$$–$$$$$

~Capitola Venetian Hotel

This historic hotel provides a touch of Italy on the beach in charming Capitola village. Looking like an apartment complex with its three rows of attached buildings separated by tiny alleys, the hotel rooms are one to three bedrooms with private baths and some have private entrances. Some have fireplaces, kitchenettes, and beachfront ocean views. Steps away are the restaurants and shops, also located right on the beach.

> 1500 Wharf Rd., Capitola, CA 95010
> 800-332-2780
> www.capitolavenetian.com
> $–$$$$

Monterey Peninsula

Moss Landing
~Captain's Inn

This is a new two-building inn, and, although one of the buildings was built in 1906, the other is new with a nautical "boathouse" theme. Each of the ten rooms has a private bath with either a soaking tub or a double shower, chandeliers, antique furniture, a fireplace, and views of the channel, dunes, or the quaint street of Moss Landing, a town filled with antique stores. The inn provides a full breakfast.

> 8122 Moss Landing Rd., Moss Landing, CA 95039
> 831-633-5550

www.captainsinn.com
$$–$$$$$

San Juan Bautista
~Posada De San Juan Hotel

In San Benito county between Gilroy and Salinas sits this charming Mexican-style village with a beautiful mission and historic museum. The mission-style hotel is right in the middle of town, next to quaint shops and restaurants. The 43 rooms are elegant with high ceilings, fireplaces, balconies and many spa tubs. The hotel, with its huge, Spanish-style lobby, and the town make for an ideal retreat. Breakfast is included.

310 Fourth St., San Juan Bautista, CA 95045
831-623-4380
$–$$$

Carmel-By-The-Sea
~Sandpiper Inn By the Sea

Built in 1929, this seaside home has seventeen rooms, all individually furnished with antiques, designer fabrics, flowers, and private baths. Some of the upstairs rooms face the ocean, which is only one block away. There are beautiful gardens and a separate cottage with a fireplace. A large continental breakfast is served and afternoon and evening sherry is included and served in the warm, comfortable living-dining room.

2408 Bay View Ave., Carmel-by-the-Sea, CA 93923
800-633-6433
www.sandpiper-inn.com
$$–$$$$$

~Mission Ranch

This inn is owned by Clint Eastwood, and this is where Oprah Winfrey stays when she visits the Monterey peninsula. The main building is an 1850s farmhouse and there are a total of 31 individual rooms, all with private baths, and all are elegant. Some have ocean or mountain views, spa tubs, and fireplaces. The grounds are magnificent, flowers and lawns surround the buildings. The restaurant on the premises, with its ocean view, is excellent and has a piano bar. Continental breakfast is included, and there is a fitness center and tennis courts.

26270 Dolores St., Carmel-by-the-Sea, CA 93923
800-538-8221
www.missionranchcarmel.com
$$$–$$$$

~Vagabond's House Inn

The best part of this Tudor-style bed and breakfast is the stone court-
yard, with beautiful gardens, a waterfall, a huge oak tree, and ferns. The
eleven rooms surround the courtyard and are decorated beautifully with
antique furnishings, fresh flowers, fireplaces, and down comforters. Com-
plimentary breakfast is brought to your room.

P.O. Box 2747, Carmel-By-The-Sea, CA 93921
800-262-1262
www.vagabondshouseinn.com
$$–$$$$$

~Monte Verde Inn

A charming small bed and breakfast with ten rooms, this was a former
residence, so it has all the charm of a beautiful, old home on a quiet street a
few blocks up the hill from the beach. One room has a kitchen, one has a
sitting room, some have fireplaces and decks, but all are cozy and comfortable and breakfast is included.

P.O. Box 394, Carmel-By-The-Sea, CA 93921
800-328-7707
$$–$$$

~Pine Inn

The historic and charming Pine Inn was built in 1889, and its 49 rooms
are a bit small, but quite cozy, with private baths, feather beds, armoires,
some ocean views, and period furnishings. The library and lobby on the main
floor are warm and comfortable decorated in tones of red and gold, with lots
of wood and antiques. The Il Fornaio restaurant is on the premises.

P.O. Box 250, Carmel-By-The-Sea, CA 93921
800-228-3851
www.pine-inn.com
$$$–$$$$$

Carmel Highlands
~Tickle Pink Inn

You'll get some of the most spectacular ocean views on California's coast from the balconies of these 35 rooms and suites, high upon the cliffs. All the rooms are elegantly-appointed, with private baths, robes, refrigerators, coffee, soft pink and beige décor, TV, phones, and all the amenities of any fine hotel, although it looks more like a two-story motel. The ocean, famous cypress tree and cliff views, though, make this unlike anyplace you have ever stayed. Breakfast and home-baked cookies, and a wine and cheese reception are included in the room price and are served in a covered, outdoor patio above the cliffs overlooking the Pacific Ocean and there is a spa tucked away in the back, against a hill. There is also a separate two-bedroom cottage with full kitchen.

155 Highland Dr., Carmel Highlands, CA 93923
800-635-4774
www.ticklepinkinn.com
$$$$$

Pacific Grove
~Borg's Ocean Front Motel

This is a pretty standard sixty-room motel, except for the views from the front half of the motel, which look out over Lover's Point and the Pacific Ocean between Monterey and Pebble Beach. There are queen, king and twin beds, desks, or a table to work on, cable TV, and phones but the reason to stay here is for the reasonable rates, and the great ocean view.

635 Ocean View Blvd., Pacific Grove, CA 93950
831-375-2406
$-$$

~Grand View Inn

A fabulous mansion, built in 1910 by Pacific Grove's first female mayor, this elegant inn has ten luxurious rooms, all with private marble baths, hardwood floors, antique furnishings, and most have incredible ocean views directly across the street. Breakfast and afternoon tea, served in the oak-columned parlor room overlooking the Pacific and the lovely gardens, is included in the room price.

557 Ocean View Blvd., Pacific Grove, CA 93950
831-372-4341
www.pginns.com
$$$–$$$$$

Monterey

~Monterey Plaza Hotel

This magnificent 290-room hotel sits directly on top of Monterey Bay. Every detail is luxurious, from the elegant lobby with views of the bay, to the restaurants, shops, and galleries on the ground floor, to the spacious rooms. Especially nice are the corner rooms, with balconies perched on pilings above the water so the only sound you hear is the lapping waves underneath, or maybe the squawking of a sea gull or seal. Bathrooms are marble, with all the amenities, and there are desks facing the ocean view. Rooms have phones, data ports, TV, and all the services of a major, luxury hotel, including room service. The Cannery shops, restaurants, and the world famous aquarium are just a few steps away if you can bring yourself to leave your wonderful room. Spa services are available.

400 Cannery Row, Monterey, CA 93940
800-368-2468
www.woodsidehotels.com
$$$$–$$$$$

~Monterey Beach Hotel/Best Western

The best views directly out to the ocean from the beach are to be found at this Best Western motel, which sits on the beach. Erosion has caused some of the back of the motel to wash away, but there is still a pool, spa, and restaurant with fabulous views. A bar in the lobby is lavishly decorated with unique art and antique furnishings. All of the rooms are good-sized. Ask for a room near the end of the hallways. You don't want to be distracted by people walking by your room. Rooms are standard motel rooms, with tables by the windows to work at, data ports, private baths, and a full breakfast at the motel's restaurant is included. It is a short drive to downtown shops and restaurants.

2600 Sand Dunes Dr.
Monterey, CA 93940
800-242-8627
$$–$$$$$

A LOT OF CLAMS, BUT WORTH IT

I like to sit on the bed in my room at the Monterey Plaza Hotel, looking out at the sea lions eating their clams, watching the kayaks and not see any people except for room service for at least 48 hours. Give yourself at least two nights here, or more if you can afford it. There are no cares, no bothers, and total comfort.

The corner rooms are especially wonderful with desks and tables looking out at the ocean and beyond. The décor is quietly luxurious, not glitzy or obtrusive, and the staff takes great care of you and your needs. Order Häagen-Dazs ice cream, but only order room service twice a day for minimal interruption.

Bring the following with you: yellow pads, good pens, a laptop computer, a box of notes or research materials, comfortable clothes like you wear around the house at night, a shawl for warmth when out on the balcony, coffees, hot chocolate packets, or teas you like best, cheeses and snacks to put in the room refrigerator, and bubble bath.

—*Elizabeth Pomada, author and literary agent (Larsen-Pomada Agency)*

Soledad: The Pinnacles National Monument
~*Inn at the Pinnacles*

This new bed and breakfast sits high up in the hills overlooking the Salinas Valley and Steinbeck country, next to Chalone Vineyards. It has six lovely rooms, all with private patios and spa tubs. This is one of the quietest out-of-the-way locations you can find. Since it is not close to restaurants, carry some food along with you.

32025 Stonewall Canyon, Soledad, CA 93960
831-678-2400
www.inatthepinnacles.com
$$–$$$

Big Sur
~*Big Sur Lodge*

This lodge, on top of a hill surrounded by the Santa Lucia Mountains and in the Pfeiffer Big Sur State Park, has 61 cottages, some attached and others separate with kitchens. All have private baths, desks or tables, most

Inn at the Pinnacles, Soledad, CA. Perched high above the Salinas Valley, known as the salad bowl of America, this bed and breakfast is adjacent to the award-winning Chalone Vineyards winery. Courtesy of Andrea Brown

have fireplaces and cathedral ceilings, and none has TV or radio, so there is nothing to stop you from writing. There is a heated pool, trails for walking, a restaurant, and a shop on the park grounds.

> 47225 Hwy. One, Big Sur, CA 93920
> 800-424-4787
> www.Bigsurlodge.com
> $–$$$

~Lucia Lodge

At Lucia Point, about 22 miles south of Big Sur valley and 38 miles north of Hearst Castle, sits this epitome of a hideaway. The ten attached, rustic cottages, with down comforters for the chilly nights, are perched on top of a cliff sticking out into the Pacific Ocean with views of the whole coastline as well as straight out to sea, and there are no TVs or radios to distract you. There is a stone bench at the cliff's edge to watch the ocean and stars at night—better than a planetarium. Continental breakfast is included at the restaurant on the premises. There is also a small general store, but bring all supplies with you.

> 62400 Hwy. One at Lucia Point, Big Sur, CA 93920
> 866-424-4787
> www.lucialodge.com
> $$–$$$$$

Lucia Lodge, Big Sur, CA. A rustic and romantic motel, about as away from it all as you can get, with absolutely the best, most dramatic ocean and mountain views anywhere. Courtesy and copyright Richard R. Hansen.

The Central Valley

Fresno

~Piccadilly Inn-Airport

This is a two-story motel that feels more like a small hotel in the central valley with nicely-landscaped grounds, a pool, a spa, a fitness room, two restaurants and a lounge. The 185 comfortable rooms have private baths, TVs, phones, desks or tables. You should ask for an upstairs room with a refrigerator and balcony facing the pool, so you won't hear the airplanes from the nearby Fresno-Yosemite International Airport.

5115 E. McKinley, Fresno, CA 93727
559-251-6000
$-$$$

WHERE GOD LIVES

The place where I get instant inspiration, every time, is Big Sur. Granted, there are problems. Technology doesn't function as completely here, but it is where God lives. And every one of the hotels, from the cheapest and least luxurious to the most sublime is a place to both soothe the soul and focus the spirit.

Big Sur is where the mountains literally meet the sea, with tiny beaches scattered a few hundred feet below Highway One.

The highway runs along the coast for about sixty miles from Carmel to Cambria with the most breathtaking views on earth. It is a remote place, where few people live. There are almost no places to get gas or anything else. Big Sur inspires with visions that impress on most people how insignificant we all are, and for a writer the challenge is to prove that it ain't so!

There are several places to stay in Big Sur, ranging from incredibly expensive (Post Ranch Inn and Ventana) to inexpensive (River Inn and Big Sur Lodge). The best value—and the one that will best force your focus to writing or painting—is Lucia Lodge. There is no television, no telephone. The only noises you hear are the ocean waves crashing 300 feet below. On clear nights, you can see shooting stars because there are no city lights nearby.

The best spot for writing is the stone bench at the edge of the cliff, overlooking the water and coast. You won't get cell phone reception here. You will be truly alone.

—*David Spiselman, CEO of CyclopsMedia.com, (www.cyclopsmedia.com), e-book publisher*

The Central Coast

Paso Robles
~Villa Toscana Bed and Breakfast

If you are dying to go to Italy but it is just too far, go instead to Villa Toscana at the Martin & Weyrich Winery, and you will feel like you are in Tuscany. This newly built, stone villa is extraordinary with its authentic Italian details, tiled floors, beamed ceilings, not to mention the large, elegant rooms named after the wines. A gourmet breakfast is included along with wines from the winery, and all the rooms have lovely vineyard vistas. There is also a separate 2-bedroom suite residence with private garage, patio, spa and fine art and furnishings. This is truly a unique getaway in this central coast wine region, with over 70 other wineries in the area.

4230 Buena Vista, Paso Robles, CA 93446
805-238-5600
www.myvillatoscana.com
$$$$$

~Creekside Bed & Breakfast

This cozy, wood cabin is a mix of the old West and the comforts of home, with a one-bedroom cottage available, including a private bath with shower, queen bed with quilt, wood walls and ceiling, a full kitchen, gas fireplace by the sitting area, and complimentary wine, fruit, cheese and breakfast included.

5325 Vineyard Dr., Paso Robles, CA 93446
805-227 6585
$$

Cambria

~Cambria Pines Lodge

This lodge on 25 acres of woods, with gazebos and gardens, has 125 rooms that are comfortable and well-appointed and some have fireplaces. A complimentary breakfast is provided and the lodge offers an indoor pool and spa, nightly entertainment, and a restaurant.

2905 Burton Dr., Cambria, CA 93428
800-445-6868
www.cambriapineslodge.com
$$–$$$$$

~Blue Dolphin Inn

An eighteen-room inn with English country décor, offering individualized room styles, some private baths, custom made furniture, refrigerators, fireplaces, and TV/VCRs, this inn has some rooms with canopy beds, spa tubs, and spectacular ocean views. The charming tea room serves a complimentary breakfast and afternoon tea. Moonstone Beach is across from the inn. There are a number of nice motels and inns, some with great ocean views, along this whole stretch of beachfront.

> 6470 Moonstone Beach Dr., Cambria, CA 93428
> 805-927-3300
> www.cambriahotels.com
> $–$$$$

San Luis Obispo
~Bridge Creek Inn

Set in the Edna Valley wine region, this tranquil bed and breakfast is a Craftsman style inn on ten acres, built in the 1970s with two elegant rooms; one has a spa tub, and the other has a clawfoot tub. Both have TV/DVD, phones. Breakfast is included.

> 5300 Righetti Rd., San Luis Obispo, CA 93401
> 805-544-3003
> www.BridgecreekInn.com
> $$$

~Madonna Inn

This 109-room inn has become a Central Coast landmark and people either love it or hate it. No two rooms are alike, and the Swiss-looking fairytale architecture of the outside is extremely unique. Avoid this inn if you dislike pink or red. There are lovely gardens, a restaurant, bakery, and shops. Some rooms have cave-like or stone walls—even in the shower, and some have velvet red furnishings or a safari theme. This imaginative inn may help get those creative juices flowing.

> 100 Madonna Rd., San Luis Obispo, CA 93405
> 800-543-9666
> www.madonnainn.com
> $$$–$$$$$

Los Osos
~Back Bay Inn

This 13-room, secluded, waterfront inn sits in Baywood Park at the south end of Morro Bay near the state park. Most of the rooms have water views and all are comfortably and individually furnished. Some rooms have kitch-enettes. Continental breakfast is included.

> 1391 Second St., Baywood Park, CA 93402
> 877-330-2225
> www.backbayinn.com
> $$–$$$$

Pismo Beach
~Pismo Beach Hotel
Originally built in 1937 as an escape for Hollywood stars like Clark Gable, Fred Astaire, Judy Garland, Spencer Tracy, Marilyn Monroe and Joan Crawford, this four-story hotel was totally renovated in 2000. Located on the main street, half a block away from the ocean, the rooms here have HBO, fireplaces, oak furniture, some suites have spa tubs, and the hotel has a homey feel that puts it one notch above a motel room. There is a pleasant courtyard and continental breakfast is included.

> 230 Pomeroy Ave., Pismo Beach, CA 93449
> 866-776-6224
> www.thepismobeachhotel.com
> $–$$$$$

~Best Western Shore Cliff Lodge
This is a large motel with the best views on this part of the central coast. Each of the 99 rooms has a fabulous ocean view, with a private balcony, a microwave, refrigerator and private bath. The motel is perched on the cliffs overlooking the Pacific and there are great ocean views from the pool and spa. The views make this anything but a typical motel, and recent renovations make it quite comfortable. There is a restaurant on the premises.

> 2555 Price St., Pismo Beach, CA 93449
> 800-441-8885
> www.shorecliff.com
> $$–$$$

Santa Barbara
~Cabrillo Inn at the Beach
This is your typical motel, but it has fabulous, open views of the ocean and the beach at the south end of the main beach strip. There is also a sepa-

rate cottage next door with two bedrooms and a full kitchen. Regular rooms have such basics as private baths, desks, and TVs. Continental breakfast is included and there are two pools, one heated. Furnishings are a bit dated and it's not as nice as the more upscale motels and hotels on the block, like the Santa Barbara Inn, but just gaze out of your room window and you won't care. The best views are from the top floor suite with its own private deck and kitchenette.

931 E. Cabrillo Blvd., Santa Barbara, CA 93103
800-648-6708
www.cabrillo-inn.com
$–$$$$

~Casa del Mar Inn

Literally across the street from the beach and near shops and restaurants, this Mediterranean-style inn has 21 rooms with some two-bedroom suites available. There are queen and king rooms, all with private baths, cable TV, mini-kitchens, fireplaces, desks, data ports, modem hook-ups, and on the grounds there are lovely gardens, sundecks, and a spa. This inn feels like a small hotel. A full breakfast and wine and cheese are included.

18 Bath St., Santa Barbara, CA 93101
800-433-3097
www.casadelmar.com
$$$–$$$$$

~Simpson House Inn

This is an award-winning historic landmark Victorian estate, built in 1874. Located on an acre of beautifully-manicured fountains and gardens in a quiet, residential neighborhood, the seven rooms are individually decorated with upscale antiques, flowered wallpaper, charming detailing, and some have decks or bay windows, sitting areas, and all but one have private baths. The common rooms downstairs are elegant, with oriental rugs, antique wood furnishings, fine art, orchids, and a magnificent dining room, serving coffee, iced tea, lemonade, wine and appetizers, cookies and sherry throughout the day. A full breakfast is served and presented with fine sterling in the privacy of your room or on the porch. All food is included and the service is perfect.

The wraparound porch has comfortable white wicker furniture overlooking the gardens. Some rooms outside of the main building have spa tubs and private entrances and patios.

121 E. Arrellaga, Santa Barbara, CA 93101
800-676-1280
www.simpsonhouseinn.com
$$$$–$$$$$

Simpson House Inn, Santa Barbara, CA. Besides beautifully decorated unique rooms, the sumptuous breakfasts and happy hours, complete with local wines and homemade appetizers, are enough to keep you from ever desiring to leave the premises. Courtesy of Andrea Brown

~San Ysidro Ranch

Tucked into the gorgeous hills of Montecito, this ranch/hotel sits on over 500 acres of coastal landscape overlooking the ocean from high above. Jackie and President John F. Kennedy spent their honeymoon here in one of the 38 rooms and cottages, which are spread out around the hills; some have private decks, most have private spas or hot tubs, private baths, fireplaces, and all have the impeccable service and the luxurious amenities of a fine hotel. There is a heated pool, tennis court, fitness center, hiking trails, organic gardens, as well as an excellent restaurant, but this is the kind of place in which you can hideaway comfortably, with no one to bother you, if that is what you want.

900 San Ysidro Ln., Santa Barbara, CA 93108
800-368-6788
www.sanysidroranch.com
$$$$$

~The Biltmore—Four Season Resort

Just below the town of Montecito on the ocean along "America's Riviera" is the magnificent Biltmore resort built on twenty acres of tropical flora. There are 210 rooms and private cottages, all with private, elegant baths, robes, safes, newspapers delivered to room, and all have upscale, elaborate décor. The management's attention to detail shows with high-speed Internet access, full room-service, and all the services and luxury one would expect at a Four Seasons Hotel. There are two pools, tennis courts, a fitness center, spa services, and wonderful restaurants. Walking into the lounge and the lobby makes you feel like you are entering an elaborate Mexican hacienda

1260 Channel Dr., Santa Barbara, CA 93108
800-332-3442, In Canada: 800-268-62-82
$$$$$

Montecito

~Montecito Inn

Montecito is a beautiful, upscale town, just south of Santa Barbara, where Oprah Winfrey has her California home. This historic small hotel with only sixty rooms and suites was built in 1928 by silent screen star

Charlie Chaplin as a place for his friends to escape to from Hollywood. In the 1950s, the hotel was renovated and gardens, a pool, spa, sauna, and a parking facility were added. All the rooms are elegant and have private baths. Some have Italian marble bathrooms with spa tubs, refrigerators, custom fireplaces, and cable TV. A complete library of Charlie Chaplin films and VCR are available. Rooms have desks or tables, phone, and data ports, Other business services are available. Complimentary breakfast is included and there is restaurant on the premises although all the town's shops and restaurants are only steps away. Pets are allowed.

1295 Coast Village Rd., Santa Barbara, CA 93108
800-843-2017
www.montecitoinn.com
$$$$–$$$$$

Summerland
~Inn on Summer Hill

This two-story country-style bed and breakfast is located between Santa Barbara and Ventura and has wonderful ocean views from rooms on the second floor. The charming rooms have fireplaces, private baths with spa tubs, canopy beds, antique furnishings, tables, TV/VCRs, stereos, balconies or patios. Complimentary breakfast, wine, appetizers and snacks are served. There is an outdoor spa. Beach access is across the freeway. Special weekday packages are available.

2520 Lillie Ave., Summerland, CA 93067
800-845-5566
www.innonsummerhill.com
$$$$$

Solvang
~The Solvang Gardens Lodge

Located at the edge of this charming, Danish-styled village, this country inn is a quiet retreat away from the main streets yet only a few blocks walk to all the shops and restaurants. There are 22 rooms with names such as "Magnolia, Butterfly Orchid, Wild Poppy, Jasmine," all have private baths, some have private decks, knotty pine paneling, fireplaces, and kitchens. Gardens surround the rooms and there are views of the mountains.

293 Alisal Rd., Solvang, CA 93463
805-688-4404
www.solvangardens.com
$–$$$

~The Chimney Sweep Inn

Old world charm is evident when you see this inn located directly in
Tivoli Square in the middle of Solvang. There are seven rooms and some
private cottages and each is individually decorated, some with lofts, some
with fireplaces. There is cable TV/HBO, coffee, telephone and continental
breakfast is included in the price. Some have spa tubs and kitchens.

1564 Copenhagen Dr., Solvang, CA 93463
800-824-6444
www.chimneysweepinn.com
$$–$$$$$

Ballard

~The Ballard Inn

This elegant inn is in the heart of Santa Barbara's wine country. With
fifteen charming rooms reflecting the area's character and local history, all
have private baths. This inn has a wonderful restaurant.

2436 Baseline Ave. Ballard, CA 93463
800-638-2466
www.ballardinn.com
$$$$–$$$$$

Santa Ynez

~Santa Ynez Inn

This beautiful mansion is located in the Santa Barbara wine country in
the tiny town and valley of Santa Ynez. There are fourteen spacious and
elegant rooms with antiques and furnishings throughout, private luxurious
baths with robes, dual telephones with data ports and voice mail, TV/DVD/
CD, coffee, air conditioning and many rooms have fireplaces, refrigerators,
balconies, bay windows, and spa tubs. Complimentary full breakfast, evening
wine, appetizers and desserts are served in the magnificent downstairs parlor rooms.

3627 Sagunto St., Santa Ynez, CA 93460
800-643, 5774
www.santaynezinn.com
$$$$$

Southern California

Ojai

~Moon's Nest Inn

This charming, scenic town is located high up in the hills above Santa Barbara and Ventura and worth the drive. This seven-room inn, including five rooms with private baths, was Ojai's first schoolhouse and each room is different. Some have open-air balconies and all overlook lovely gardens and a pond. A full breakfast is included.

210 E. Matilija St., Ojai, CA 93023
805-646-6635
www.moonsnestinn.com
$$–$$$

Venice

~The Venice Beach House

This turn-of-the-century mansion is one block from Venice Beach. There are nine elegant rooms and suites, most with private baths and all with desks. A full breakfast and evening refreshments are included and served in the downstairs parlor rooms with window seats, antique furnishings, and views of the gardens and porch. One room has an ocean view, a couple rooms have balconies and a few of them are rather small but all are decorated beautifully with wicker or period pieces and contain TVs. In the midst of all the beach activities that make Venice Beach such fun, this is a little slice of heaven.

#15 Thirtieth Ave., Venice, CA 90291
310-823-1966
$$–$$$$

Santa Monica

~Shutters on the Beach

It doesn't get any better than this. The 198 rooms are the ultimate in luxury and elegance with some of the best ocean views anywhere in the country. There is a fabulous restaurant on the premises and the service is impeccable.

> 1 Pico Blvd., Santa Monica, CA 90405
> 800-334-9000
> www.shuttersonthebeach.com
> $$$$$

~Channel Road Inn

Named by many travel magazines as one of the best bed and breakfast inns in the West, this historic manor was built in 1915 and has been restored beautifully. It is one block away from the beach in Santa Monica Canyon and has fourteen rooms, all individualized and all have private baths. Some rooms have fireplaces, all have TV/VCRs, data ports, robes, and other up-scale details. A few of the rooms have ocean views. A full breakfast is included and there is an outside spa.

> 219 W. Channel Rd., Santa Monica, CA 90402
> 310-459-1920
> www.channelroadinn.com
> $$$–$$$$$

West Hollywood
~Le Montrose Suite Hotel

This all-suite hotel has recently undergone a 2.5 million-dollar renovation and all the 132 suites are decorated with a European-style motif and include private baths, sunken living room areas, kitchenettes, balconies TV/VCR's, data ports, multi-line phones for Internet access and all the amenities of a fine hotel. There is a rooftop pool, spa, cabana, and tennis court with fabulous views, as well as a fitness center. The hotel's restaurant is called "The Library." Close to Beverly Hills and Sunset Strip, this is a little oasis in the middle of Los Angeles.

> 900 Hammond St., West Hollywood, CA 90069
> 310-855-1115
> www.Lemontrose.com
> $$$$–$$$$$

Hollywood
~Chateau Marmont
A historic hotel since 1929, this hotel is in the hills off Sunset Boulevard. Its 63 rooms, suites, bungalows, and cottages have a castle-like feel, with painted ceilings, full kitchens, private baths and terraces or patios, living and dining rooms, and lots of original tile. The lobby, courtyard restaurant and beautiful gardens take you back to the elegant golden days of Hollywood.

8221 Sunset Blvd, Hollywood, CA 90046
323-656-1010
www.designhotels.com
$$$$–$$$$$

Long Beach
~Dockside Boat & Bed
Maybe your idea of the perfect escape is to hide out aboard your own yacht. At this unusual inn; four boats are available for rent at this private dock and even a continental breakfast is included. San Francisco and Oakland venues have the same deal. The boats are fully furnished with all the basics, and there are shops and restaurants nearby.

316 E. Shoreline Dr., Long Beach, CA 90802
562-436-3111
www.boatandbed.com
$$$$–$$$$$

Seal Beach
~The Seal Beach Inn
This country inn, one block from the beach, has an old-world charm, with its Mediterranean-style courtyard with fountains and gardens. The historic inn has 23 elegant rooms and suites with private baths, canopy beds, antique furnishings, and fresh flowers. Breakfast and afternoon tea are included, and it is a short walk to the many restaurants and shops in this quaint seaside town.

212 5th St., Seal Beach, CA 90740
800-Hideaway
www.sealbreachinn.com
$$$–$$$$$

Dana Point
~Blue Lantern Inn
This is a Four Sisters Inn with beautiful views from its Cliffside location overlooking the Pacific Ocean. Each of the 29 large rooms features a spa tub, fireplace, TV/VCR, sitting areas and luxurious furnishings and amenities. Some rooms have private decks or balconies with ocean views, and there are some tower rooms with champagne and chocolates included. Downstairs, there is a charming dining room, parlor, and library, where breakfast and afternoon wine and appetizers are served.

> 34343 St. of the Blue Lantern, Dana Point, CA 92629
> 800-950-1236
> **$$$–$$$$$**

San Clemente
~Casa Tropicana
This five-story Spanish style inn was built in 1990, and its nine different rooms with private baths are named and themed after Paradise Island resorts and many have fireplaces, ocean views, and spa tubs, and all have modern conveniences. A full breakfast, champagne and treats are included and served on the ocean-view patio.

> 610 Avenida Victoria, San Clemente, CA 92672
> 800-492-1245
> www.casatropicana.com
> **$$–$$$$$**

Laguna Beach
~Eiler's Inn
This 12-room inn looks more like it should be in New Orleans than California, but it is charming with its gardens and fountains throughout the courtyard, and its well-appointed rooms are cozy and European-looking in style, with private baths. Breakfast and wine and cheese are included.

> 741 S. Coast Hwy., Laguna Beach, CA 92651
> 866-617-2696
> www.lagunabeach.com/eilersinn
> **$$–$$$$**

~By-the-Sea Inn

Many of this inn's 36 rooms have wonderful ocean view balconies, some kitchenettes, all have private baths, all have the basic amenities, and a complimentary continental breakfast is included. There is a pool, spa and sauna, and it is only a three-block walk to the charming shops and restaurants of downtown Laguna Beach.

> 475 N. Coast Hwy., Laguna Beach, CA 92651
> 800-297-0007
> www.lagunabeach.com/bytheseainn
> $–$$$$

Greater San Diego

Temecula
~Loma Vista Bed & Breakfast

Located in southern California's wine country, this Spanish mission-style inn situated on a hillside, boasts six individually decorated rooms with antiques throughout and private baths. Some have balconies with views of the local vineyards. A complimentary champagne breakfast, wine, and evening beverages are served.

> 33350 La Serena Wy., Temecula, CA 92591
> 909-676-7047
> $$–$$$

Del Mar
~L'Auberge Del Mar

Located on a hillside above the ocean, this elegant and upscale three-story hotel has 120 rooms, some with ocean and coastal views, some with balconies and all with luxurious private baths, robes, cable TV, safes and the ultimate in pampering service. There is a pool, spa, sundecks, sauna, tennis courts, gift shops, a fine restaurant and spa services available. Superb restaurants and shops are located across the street in this beautiful, seaside town.

> 1540 Camino, Del Mar, CA 92014
> 858-259-1515, 800-245-9157

www.delmarspa.com
$$$$$

La Jolla
~The Bed and Breakfast Inn at La Jolla

This magnificent inn, a block from the beach has fifteen elegant rooms with private baths, canopy beds, fresh fruit, flowers and sherry, oriental rugs and fine art. Furnishings are in soft tones, with period furnishings and chaise lounges or comfortable sitting areas. A full candlelit breakfast and afternoon refreshments are included. The beautiful seaside village shops and restaurants are steps away.

> 7753 Draper Ave., La Jolla, CA 92037
> 800-582-2466
> www.Innlajolla.com
> $$$–$$$$$

~Redwood Hollow Cottages

This is a registered historic site with eleven cottages, studios, homes and apartments dating from 1915 through the 1940s with rustic, yet comfortable furnishings including kitchens and fireplaces around the corner from the beach. There are gardens and some cottages have private patios and all are close to the shops and restaurants in town. This is a great place for a longer stay in southern California.

> 256 Prospect St., La Jolla, CA 92037
> 858-459-8747
> www.redwoodhollow-lajolla.com
> $$$–$$$$$

~The Lodge at Torrey Pines

This is a beautiful and luxurious hotel with 175 large rooms and suites with private baths that have granite counters and soaking tubs, Stickley-style furnishings, workspaces, high-speed Internet access. Some rooms have balconies, fireplaces, and views of the ocean. Attention has been given to every detail. The lodge is next to the championship Torrey Pines golf course. It was built with beautiful wood and stone and has an elegant lobby, restaurants, full-service spa and all business services.

11480 N. Torrey Pines Rd., La Jolla, CA 92037
858-453-4420
www.lodgetorreypines.com
$$$$$

~Hotel La Jolla

Located right in the middle of town, but next to the beach, this is a small hotel recently underwent a $14 million renovation. It has lovely, old-fashioned rooms yet all have the modern basic amenities. There is an ocean-view restaurant, a pool and a fitness center. There is great service here for when you feel the need to be pampered.

7955 La Jolla Shores Dr., La Jolla, CA 92037
858-459-0261
www.hotellajolla.com
$$$$–$$$$$

Coronado (San Diego)
~Hotel Del Coronado

This is a famous landmark and historic hotel across the Coronado Bridge from downtown San Diego. It is a must-see if you visit the area, whether you stay here or not. Located on the beach, the Victorian-style 600-plus rooms, turn-of-the-century inn has magnificent views, wonderful restaurants and shops, decks, gardens, a pool, a spa, a fitness room, spa services, and everything one could possibly desire or need. Rooms are elegant, with nods to the period in furnishings, but also including all the conveniences of modern hotels with TV, phones, data ports, luxurious private baths, and desks.

1500 Orange Ave., Coronado, CA 92118
800-Hotel-Del
www.Hoteldel.com
$$$$$

San Diego
~Pacific Terrace Hotel

This is the only four-star hotel located directly on the beach,. It has beautiful ocean views from room balconies, upscale motel-like furnishings, phones, TV, data ports, robes, coffee, and private baths, some with spa tubs. There is an ocean-view pool and spa. Continental breakfast is complimentary.

> 610 Diamond St., San Diego, CA 92109
> 800-848-5916
> www.pacificterrace.com
> $$$$$

Hotel Del Coronado, San Diego, CA. Built right on the beach on Coronado Island, expansive ocean views from this elegant, historic hotel can be found from just about anywhere on the lavish grounds. Courtesy of the Hotel Coronado

~A Victorian Heritage Park Bed & Breakfast Inn

Located in the historic part of Old Town San Diego, this award-winning inn is a beautifully-restored Queen Anne mansion with twelve elegant rooms, including featherbeds, antique furnishings, some with clawfoot tubs or spa tubs in the private baths, and a full candlelit breakfast is included, as well as afternoon tea on the large veranda.

> 2470 Heritage Park Row, San Diego, CA 92110
> 800-995-2470

www.heritageparkinn.com
$$–$$$$$

Palm Springs

~Ingleside Inn

Built in 1925 as a home and converted to an inn in 1935, this historic landmark building has 30 suites, villas, and mini-suites with private baths, fireplaces, refrigerators stocked with free snacks and drinks, private terraces, and some rooms have private spa tubs and steam baths. This is an elegant inn with the feel of the old days of splendor, right in the heart of the beautiful city of Palm Springs, close to everything.

200 W. Ramon Rd., Palm Springs, CA 92264
800-772-6652
www.Inglesideinn.com
$$–$$$$$

IT'S 120 DEGREES OUTSIDE!

I like to escape to Santa Barbara and Santa Inez—often. But I stay with friends, so you can't go there. They are my friends. However, a lot of my writers go to Palm Springs in the summer and lock themselves in air-conditioned rooms and write.

This works well, because they sure aren't going to go out into the 120 degree temperatures. And, when you choose to go to Palm Springs during the summer months, the family doesn't want to go with you, so you can really be alone to get some work done.

—Andy Cohen, president of Grade A Entertainment, representing writers in Los Angeles

~Willows Historic Palm Springs Inn

This eight-room inn, where Clark Gable, Carol Lombard, and Albert Einstein stayed, has been totally restored to recreate the charm and elegance of a Mediterranean-style villa right in the old part of downtown Palm Springs. All rooms have private baths, antiques, cable TV, phones, and refrigerators, and some have fabulous mountain views. The grounds are beautiful featuring gardens, a waterfall, and a pool. A full breakfast is included.

412 W. Tahquitz Canyon, Palm Springs, CA 92262
800-966-9597
www.thewillowspalmsprings.com
$$$$–$$$$$

Julian
~Orchard Hill Country Inn

In the heart of historic Julian, established in the 1800s, this bed and breakfast features 22 rooms in several different buildings, some lodge-like, others in Craftsman cottages, and all set against a hillside with trees, gardens with hammocks, and walking trails all around. All rooms have private baths, antique furnishings, TV/VCRs, and some have fireplaces, porches and spa tubs. A full breakfast, fresh-baked cookies, and beverages are all included, and there is an excellent restaurant on the grounds.

2502 Washington St., Julian, CA 92036
800-71-ORCHARD
www.orchardhill.com
$$$$–$$$$$

HAWAII & ALASKA

Hawaii

Our forty-ninth and fiftieth states are filled with scenic wonders such as volcanoes, waterfalls, glaciers, and wildlife. There are amazing views wherever you look. There may be too many diversions to make these places ideal escapes, but here are some special spots if your heart yearns to be in these fabulous states.

Big Island or Hawaii

Volcano Village
~Chalet Kilauea, The Inn at Volcano

Kilauea is a must see in Hawaii, as it is the only active volcano in the country. This twelve-unit inn has some suites, rooms, and homes available and is right across the highway from the Volcanoes National Park and is surrounded by an ancient fern forest. Each of the units is unique with themes from the owner's travels all over the world, and all have private, marble baths with spa tubs, tropical flowers, TV/VCR, phone, and elegant furnishings. A complimentary candlelit breakfast is available, as well as afternoon tea and Kona coffee liqueur by the grand fireplace in the lobby. Though this is Hawaii, evenings get chilly.

> Volcano Village, Box 998, HI 96785
> 800-937-7786
> www.volcano-hawaii.com
> **$$$–$$$$$**

Volcanoes National Park
~Volcano House

You can actually stay at a historic hotel on the rim of a volcano, with many of the 42 rooms looking into the lunar-like crater. Rooms are basic, with private baths, although the inn is charming in an old-fashioned way. There is no air conditioning but it is hardly ever necessary. There is a bar and restaurant with amazing views of the forests and crater.

Box 53, Volcano, HI 96718
808-967-7321
$–$$$

Hilo

~Hilo Bay Hotel

Also known as "Uncle Billy's" this unique four-story hotel on Hilo bay has 142 rooms, but ask for the corner rooms that lie directly above the waters, particularly the upper floor rooms that include balconies. Other rooms lie along a lushly-landscaped outdoor courtyard with ponds and some have bay/ocean views. Huge banyan trees line the front of the hotel. There is a Polynesian-style restaurant, a bar, a pool and a sign in the lobby that expresses the funky Hawaiian spirit of the place stating: "In case of tsunami 1) Remain calm 2) Pay bill 3) Run like hell."

87 Banyan Dr., Hilo, HI 96720
808-935-0861
$$–$$$$

~Shipman House Bed & Breakfast Inn

Listed on the National Register of Historic Places this beautiful Victorian inn was built in 1899 and author Jack London stayed here. There are five bedrooms, and all, except one have a private bath, and the inn is filled with fine antiques, oriental rugs, and Douglas fir floors so shoes are kept outside. Rooms have no televisions, phones, or other distractions and a large, continental breakfast is included and served overlooking the inn's rainforest gulch.

131 Ka'iulani St., Hilo, HI 96720
800-627-8447
www.Shipmanhouse.com
$$$$

Waikoloa

~Waikoloa Villas

Located at the top of seven beautifully-landscaped acres, overlooking the ocean, next to a Robert Trent golf course, these three-story one to three bedroom condominium units include a pool, spa and nearby tennis courts. All are

comfortably furnished with full kitchens, private baths with linens and tow-
els, living rooms with TV, and furnished terraces or balconies.

Box 385134, Waikoloa Village Station, HI 96738
800-535-0085
$–$$$$$

Kailua-Kona
~Kona Village Resort

These 125 rooms/suites are one or two-room thatched "hales," or bungalows, surrounded by palm trees, flowers, and the ocean. All have private
baths, a Polynesian theme, but no televisions, phones, or radios are present
to distract you from the serene beauty of the area. There are hammocks,
pools, spas, boats, tennis courts and a fitness center.

Box 1299, Kailua-Kona, HI 96740
808-325-5555
www.konavillage.com
$$$$$

The Island of Maui

Kihei
~Maui Lu Resort

One of the oldest hotels on this island, set on 28 acres of lawns, with
palm trees, lush foliage and beachfront, this place is your basic motel, except
for two buildings located right on the beach with some of the best views in
Maui. The rooms are fairly standard with private baths, TV, phone, table
and chairs, refrigerators, coffee and balconies. Ask for a room in buildings
one or two, for the most reasonable oceanfront views available on this island. The beach in front of these rooms is one of the most beautiful in Hawaii, with palm trees and views of the other islands. There is a pool and
some restaurants are within walking distance.

575 S. Kihei Rd., Kihei, HI 96753
800-922-7866
$–$$$$

~Nona Lani Cottages

There are eight cottages on two acres of lush grounds only 20 yards from the beach and some cottages have ocean views. The cottages are fully equipped with all electric kitchens, full bathrooms, private terraces, air conditioning, ceiling fans, TV, linens, and comfortable furnishings.

> 455 S. Kihei Rd., Kihei, HI 96753
> 800-733-2688
> www.Nonalanicottages.com
> $–$$

Wailea

The Wailea coast boasts most of the more upscale hotels, such as The Four Seasons, The Grand Wailea Spa & Resort, the Kea Lani and The Renaissance Hotel, all located along the most magnificent walking path in the world, stretching along the coast above spectacular beaches. These places are better for vacations than for working but the Wailea Marriot is especially conducive for inspiration and is the home of the Maui Writers Conference.

~Wailea Marriot-An Outrigger Resort

Set on 22 oceanfront acres, this may be the most beautiful location of any hotel in the country. Just about every room in this 500-room resort has an incredible ocean view and a terrace overlooking other Hawaiian islands, as well as the ocean. The entire hotel has undergone an extensive renovation and the well-appointed rooms have private baths, robes, safes, air conditioning, desks, phones with voice mail, and coffee, and there are spa services, pools, and spas overlooking the ocean and rocks below. The opulent open-air lobby has shops, a bar, and restaurants.

> 3700 Wailea Alanui Dr., Wailea, HI 96753
> 808-879-1922, 800-688-7444
> $$$–$$$$$

INSPIRATION IN PARADISE

"My favorite getaway is the Marriott Outrigger on Maui in Wailea. It's something about how quiet it is there for me. I won't tell you my favorite room, or I may never be able to get it again."

—*Jack Canfield, author of the bestselling CHICKEN SOUP series*

Wailea Marriot-Outrigger Hotel, Maui, HI. Jutting out into the ocean, this hotel has the best views of the ocean and outlying islands of all the other hotels along the magnificent Wailea coast of Maui. Courtesy of Andrea Brown

Paia

~*The Blue Tile Beach House and Spyglass House*

Stay in either a beachfront house or separate rooms/suites on the north shore of Maui only ten minutes from the airport. Fully furnished in comfortable, contemporary Hawaiian style, there are fully-equipped kitchens, private baths, and a courtyard with a sunken, tiled spa close to the water's edge. There are three houses that can be rented individually or separately, with shared common rooms. A white-sand beach is right outside the back door, but it does often get breezy.

> 367 Hana Hwy., Paia, HI 96779
> 800-475-6695
> www.spyglassmaui.com
> $$$–$$$$

Lahaina

~Hale Kai

These oceanfront vacation condominiums have 1–3 bedroom units, individually decorated with contemporary, bright furnishings and every unit has a beautiful ocean view room—some practically in the water. Full kitchens, linens, TV/VCR, ceiling fans, dishwasher, and linens are all included, and there is a pool and barbecue grill right on the beach.

> 3691 Lower Honoapiilani Rd., Lahaina, HI 96761
> 800-446-7307
> www.halekai.com.
> **$$–$$$$**

Hana

~Hotel Hana Maui

This is luxurious, ultra-deluxe hotel spread over 66 acres of hillside and gardens, with 94 rooms and cottages, most with amazing ocean views. Some of the private, rustic-looking cottages on the beach have private spas on the decks, and all rooms have elegant, yet comfortable furnishings and all the amenities of a fine hotel, but without television, radios, or clocks. Many of the staff have worked here for decades and the service at the hotel and fine restaurant is impeccable. There is a private pool and beach area, and many activities and shops are to be found both in the hotel and across the street in tiny, scenic Hana.

> P.O. Box 9, Hana, HI 96713
> 800-321-4262
> www.hotelhanamaui.com
> **$$$$$**

The Island of Oahu

Honolulu

~Colony Surf Hotel

Located right at Diamond Head, this twelve-story hotel was especially popular with artists, writers and celebrities in the 1960s and has recently been renovated with beautiful, light, airy, elegantly-appointed rooms with balconies, many facing Diamond Head. There is also a fabulous restaurant on the premises, and a continental breakfast is included.

> 2885 Kalakaua Ave., Honolulu, HI 96815
> 808-924-3111
> www.slh.com/colonysu/
> **$$$$–$$$$$**

~Manoa Valley Inn

Located near the University of Hawaii campus, this mansion dating from 1919, is listed as a National Register of Historic Places inn and has seven rooms filled with antiques and period furnishings. There are private baths, a sunroom, veranda, parlor and gardens. Breakfast, afternoon wine and refreshments are included.

> 2001 Vancouver Dr., Honolulu, HI 96822
> 800-634-5115
> www.manoavalleyinn.com
> **$$–$$$$**

The Island of Kauai

Kapaa

~Aloha Country Vacation Rentals

Located on a two-acre setting of fruit trees and gardens with mountain views, the main house has two bedrooms and several one-bedroom cottages that are available to rent. All have private baths, kitchenettes, TV, ceiling fans, linens and other necessities, but there is no maid service. This is the perfect, quiet retreat, yet it is near the shops and restaurants of Kapaa in the middle of the island.

> 505 Kamalui Rd., Kapaa, HI 96746
> 808-947-6019
> **$–$$$**

Princeville

~Hanalei Colony Resort

This northern part of Kauai is the prettiest part of the island, and there are a number of beautiful places to stay, including the Princeville Resort, an elegant, full-service hotel and resort with golf courses, restaurants and shops. The Hanalei Colony Resort is the only oceanfront condominium complex in the area and it has beautiful accommodations, mostly two-bedroom units with fully-equipped kitchens and lovely furnishings. There is a pool and spa on the premises.

> P.O. Box 206, Hanalei, HI 96714
> 800-628-3004
> $$$$–$$$$$

The Island of Lana'i

Lana'i City
~The Lodge at Koele
On this tiny island there is a beautiful and tranquil 102-room lodge up on a hill. There is also a Japanese garden, Pacific-rim fine art throughout and an English conservatory. It is easy to forget you are in Hawaii as the décor is more like a plantation estate, with wood and stone architecture. The rooms with private baths are elegant and have four-poster beds, quilts, local art and period pieces, plus all the amenities of an upscale resort. There is a restaurant, pool, spa, fitness center and a nearby beach, as well as a famous golf course.

> Box 310, Lana'i City, HI 96763
> 808-565-7300
> $$$$$

Alaska

Barrow
~King Eider Inn
This lodge is located next to the Barrow Airport and has large, comfortable rooms with pine log furniture throughout. The inn is family owned, and there are homey touches everywhere including the common rooms loaded with books, a large video library, and a sauna. Beverages are served all day.

Some rooms have kitchenettes, all have private baths, and there are complimentary coffee and homemade muffins for breakfast.

> 1752 Ahkovak St., P.O. Box 1283, Barrow, AK 99723
> 888-303-4337
> www.Kingeider.net
> $

Angoon
~Favorite Bay Inn

Right outside the Tingit Village, across from Admiralty Island, is this beautiful house with six rooms and shared baths, overlooking the bay, with forests all around it. Rooms have quilts, homemade cookies, and comfortable furnishings, and meals are taken at a nearby lodge. Serene and tranquil, this is a beautiful place to really get away from it all.

> Box 101, Angoon, AK 99820
> 800-423-3123
> www.favoritebayinn.com
> $$–$$$

Nome
~Home Nugget Inn

Located at the end of the Iditarod Trail, this 47-room lodge offers private baths and comfortable wood-paneled rooms with TVs and a restaurant, on the premises.

> Box 1470, Nome, AK 99762
> 877-443-2323
> www.homenuggetinn.com
> $$–$$$

Ketchikan
~Westcoast Cape Foe Lodge

Located a few minutes from Tongass National Forest, high up on a hill, the main way to enter this hotel is via a tram ride from downtown Ketchikan. This 72-room hotel has private baths, room service, data ports and modem connections, cable TV, coffee, along with pine-beamed ceilings that give it a warm, rustic cabin like feel, and it affords either water or mountain views. There is a restaurant and lounge on the premises.

800 Venezia Wy., Ketchikan, AK 99901
877-897-4420
www.westcoastcapefoelodge.com
$$$–$$$$

4

THE
SOUTHWEST

Nevada

Arizona

New Mexico

Utah

Texas

These states offer desert, big sky, mountain, red rock, and canyon land-scapes that many creative people find soothing. Places like Sedona, Taos, and Austin offer writers and artists much inspiration.

Nevada

Las Vegas and Reno aren't included in this book, as there are simply too many distractions. However, there are some quiet and soothing places to visit in Nevada if you are a writer or artist.

Boulder City
~*Boulder Dam Hotel*
Less than a half-hour from Las Vegas, this bed and breakfast, built in 1933 in Dutch colonial-style, is the first Nevada hotel to be accepted on the National Register of Historic Places list. The 22 rooms with private baths are furnished in period pieces and antiques, and offer air conditioning, Internet access, data ports, phones, and charming amenities. A full breakfast and wine and cheese are included in the price, and this is a non-gaming town so there aren't any distractions.

> 1305 Arizona St., Boulder City, NV 89005
> 702-293-3510
> www.boulderdamhotel.com
> $$–$$$

Incline Village
~*Inn at Incline*
Incline Village is just over the California border at Lake Tahoe and has the same spectacular scenery as other parts of the lake. This two-story, 38-room inn is surrounded by forests and is located close to the lake and town. The rooms have all the amenities of a nice motel, including balconies, an indoor pool, spa and sauna.

> 1003 Tahoe Blvd., Incline Village, NV 89451
> 800-824-6391

www.innatincline.com
$–$$$

Arizona

Sedona

~Canyon Villa Bed & Breakfast Inn

This is a great location as it is about two hours from both the Grand Canyon and Phoenix area. This award-winning inn has eleven luxurious rooms, all decorated differently, but all Mission-style with tiled floors, red-rock views, private baths with spa-tubs and robes, French doors that lead out to patios or balconies, TV/CD players, and some rooms have fireplaces. Included are a full three-course breakfast, evening appetizers, and snacks and beverages. There is a pool and spa with gorgeous red-rock views.

125 Canyon Circle Dr., Sedona, AZ 86351
800-453-1166
www.canyonvilla.com
$$$$–$$$$$

~The Inn on Oak Creek

This beautiful inn, located on a spring-fed creek, began as an art gallery and is now an eleven–room bed and breakfast. Two of the rooms are suites with decks and fabulous water views. All rooms are elegant and include private baths, spa tubs, gas fireplaces, TV/VCR, phones and robes. A gourmet breakfast and afternoon refreshments are included at this elegant inn.

556 Hwy. 179, Sedona, AZ 86336
800-499-7896
www.Sedona-inn.com
$$$$–$$$$$

~Enchantment Resort

This adobe-style inn is built into the hillside of Boynton Canyon on seventy acres in the Coconino National Forest. The 220 rooms are actually large one-or two-bedroom haciendas, built in 1987, and all are elegantly-appointed. The views are awesome and inspiring and there is a pool, healing spa, sauna, fitness center, and tennis courts. The resort restaurant is rated one of the best in the state.

> 525 Boynton Canyon Rd., Sedona, AZ 86336
> 520-282-2900
> www.slh.com/enchantm/
> **$$$$–$$$$$**

Grand Canyon
~El Tovar Hotel

A National Historic Landmark building, this hotel was built in 1905 and completely renovated in 1984. Overlooking the south rim of the canyon, the views and rooms are wonderful. These 78 accommodations with air conditioning, TV, phones and a restaurant on the premises, are the most luxurious at the canyon, although still more rustic than most other nice hotels.

> P.O. Box 699, Grand Canyon, AZ 86023
> 303-297-2757
> www.grandcanyon.com
> **$$–$$$$$**

Tucson
~Hacienda del Desierto Bed & Breakfast

The old-world charm is both inside and outside at this inn, with courtyards, flowers, and fountains and beautifully decorated Southwest-style décor inside the casitas, some with private entrances and patios. Three have kitchens, all have air conditioning, ceiling fans, private baths, TV, phone, and upscale amenities. Breakfast and refreshments are included in the room price.

> 11770 E. Rambling Trail, Tucson, AZ 85747
> 800-982-1795
> **$$–$$$$**

~The Suncatcher Bed & Breakfast

Four individual, large, lovely rooms with private baths, queen beds— some with canopies—TV/VCR, one with a fireplace and a warm, relaxing patio at which to enjoy the complimentary breakfast.

105 N. Avenida Javelina, Tucson, AZ 85748
877-775-8355
www.Thesuncatcher.com
$–$$$

New Mexico

Taos

~Casa de las Chimeneas Inn

This is "the house of chimneys", located just two blocks from the main street of charming Taos in northern New Mexico. As its name suggests, each of the eight rooms has its own fireplace/chimney, and all are individually decorated with a Southwest theme of wood beamed ceilings, tiled floors with Southwestern rugs, cable TV/HBO, private baths, fresh flowers and refrigerators stocked with free beverages. Ask for the "Library Room"—a 500 square foot suite with private walled patio, skylight, and the sitting room is an old library with wooden floors and beamed ceiling. Included in the room price is a huge three-course breakfast and an evening buffet supper. There is an outdoor spa, a magnificent courtyard with fountains and gardens, fitness room, and spa services are available.

405 Cordoba Rd., Taos, NM 87571
877-758-4777
www.visit-Taos.com
$$$–$$$$$

Albuquerque

~Hacienda Antigua Bed & Breakfast

This historic 200-year old inn, with four rooms containing private baths, fireplaces, and Southwestern theme of folk art and antiques, located near the downtown area is a wonderful blend of charm, history and warmth. There is a pool, and a full breakfast is included.

6708 Tierra Dr. NW, Albuquerque, NM 87107
800-201-2986
www.haciendantiqua.com
$$–$$$

Casa Chimeneas Inn, Taos, NM. The Spanish town of Taos, also known formally as Don Fernando de Taos, still has the working Taos pueblo open to visitors, a few minutes from this Southwestern-style inn. Courtesy of Ken Gallard

Sante Fe

~Inn of the Anasazi

This luxurious 59-room inn is located right next to the Plaza and across from museums. It has authentic adobe architecture and there are handcrafted Southwestern furnishings throughout the inn and a restaurant on the premises. All rooms have private baths and are elegantly-appointed with first class amenities. Many have kiva fireplaces.

113 Washington St., Santa Fe, NM 87501
505-988-3030
$$$$–$$$$$

~El Farolito Bed & Breakfast Inn

This inn offers eight private casitas with impeccable art and furnishings in warm earth tones, and with private baths. The authentic adobe architecture with wood beamed ceilings and private fireplaces makes this one of the most attractive inns in New Mexico. All rooms have fine linens, large wood beds, patios, TV, phone, tables and comfortable chairs, and coffee. A large continental breakfast is complimentary and is served on the back patio, and it is a short walk to the wonderful museums, galleries, and restaurants in downtown Santa Fe.

514 Galisteo St., Santa Fe, NM 87501
888-634-8782
www.farolito.com
$$$–$$$$

~Grant Corner Inn

Located in downtown, two blocks from the square, this nine-room inn has private baths and elegantly-appointed rooms, many with canopy beds and fine fabrics. This lushly-gardened bed and breakfast boasts all the luxury items necessary for a delightful stay and breakfast is a gourmet feast, with Sunday brunch available to the public as well as to the guests.

122 Grant Ave., Santa Fe, NM 87501
800-964-9003
www.grantcornerinn.com
$$$–$$$$$

~Don Gasper Inn

This is an elegant, adobe-style inn with twelve rooms, most with private baths, white shuttered windows and stylish, modern Southwestern furnishings. Rooms contain spa tubs, fireplaces, Navajo Kachina rugs, and refrigerators stocked with complimentary beverages. Breakfast is included and served in the magnificent gardens around the inn.

623 Don Gaspar, Santa Fe, NM 87505
888-986-8664
www.dongaspar.com
$$–$$$$$

~Inn of the Turquoise Bear

A historic and literary bed and breakfast, this adobe villa, entertained people such as Ansel Adams, Rita Hayworth, Errol Flynn, D.H. Lawrence, Willa Cather and Robert Frost, and guests stay in rooms named after the many former guests. There are eleven rooms and suites with private entrances and baths, surrounding a courtyard filled with flowers. Old Southwest-inspired, yet elegant, rooms have TV/VCR, phone, robes, flowers, fruit, and kiva fireplaces and some contain beamed ceilings. A large continental breakfast is included and a six-block walk brings you onto the Plaza.

> 342 E. Buena Vista St., Santa Fe, NM 87501
> 800-396-4104
> www.turquoisebear.com
> $$–$$$$

Galisteo

~Galisteo Inn

Only 23 miles southeast of Santa Fe, this Spanish colonial inn was built by the original settlers in New Mexico, and the missionary style architecture and furnishings are thematic throughout. There are twelve rooms, nine with private baths, but all have original wood-beamed ceilings, a fireplace, TV, and Southwestern artifacts. There is a pool and a spa. A full breakfast is included, and the restaurant also serves lunch and dinner.

> HC 75, Box 4, Galisteo, NM 87540
> 505-466-8200
> www.galisteoinn.com
> $–$$$$

Utah

Midway

~Homestead Resort

Located less than an hour from Salt Lake City and about 25 minutes from Park City, this hotel is set against a backdrop of the Wasatch Mountains, with mineral hot springs on the premises. The 142-room hotel with private baths and comfortable furnishings has all the amenities of a good hotel, including a pool and fitness facilities, but it is the surrounding beauty and inspiring walking trails that make this a special place.

700 N. Homestead Dr., Midway, UT 84049
888-327-7220
www.Homesteadresort.com
$$-$$$$$

Park City
~Old Miners' Lodge
There are numerous hotels and resorts in this beautiful ski resort town, but this twelve-unit lodge, built in 1889 as a boarding house for miners, is quiet and historic. Restored beautifully, all rooms have private baths and antique furnishings and there are three suites. A full breakfast and evening beverages are included and there is an outdoor spa.

615 Woodside Ave., Park City, UT 84060
800-648-8068
www.oldminerslodge.com
$-$$$$$

Salt Lake City
~La Europa Royale
This newly-built European-style small hotel located near downtown is elegant. Surrounding the hotel are ponds, gardens, and walking paths and the seven rooms are beautiful with sitting areas, desks, data ports, TV/VCR, private baths with spa tubs/separate showers, and fireplaces. There is room service, a bar, a full breakfast is included and served on the lovely patio.

1135 E. Vine St., Salt Lake City, UT. 84121
800-523-8767
www.laeuropa.com
$$$-$$$$$

~Wolfe Krest Inn
A magnificent old mansion with thirteen suites, this elegant inn has private baths with spa tubs, fireplaces, sitting areas, and beautiful, period

pieces, rugs, and furnishings throughout the rooms and dining room. Breakfast is included.

> 273 N.E. Capitol Blvd., Salt Lake City, UT 84103
> 800-669-4525
> www.wolfekrest.com
> $$$$–$$$$$

~Salt City Jail (Anniversary Inn)

The 36 rooms are all different with themes such as the "Lighthouse Room" featuring an actual lighthouse, the "Safari Room," "Egyptian Room," "Phantom of the Opera Room" and the "Red Rock Room." There are two hotels in this chain in the city, so check both out and choose the theme that will inspire you the most. All the rooms have elegant amenities, private baths, and business services, and breakfast is included.

> 460 South 1000 East and 678 East South Temple, Salt Lake City,
> UT 84102
> 800-324-4152
> www.anniversaryinn.com
> $$–$$$

Springdale: At Zion National Park

~Novel House Inn

With the sandstone cliffs and mountains of Zion National Park in the background, this literary bed and breakfast is the perfect hideaway for writers needing inspiration. The ten rooms, all with private baths, are named after such famous authors as Mark Twain, Jane Austen, Leo Tolstoy, Charles Dickens and others. All have antique wood furnishings, writing desks or tables, fireplaces, and views of the cliffs and mountains. Full breakfast is included.

> 73 Paradise Rd., Springdale, UT 84767
> 800-711-8400
> www.novelhouseinn.com
> $$

St. George

~Seven Wives Inn

Only a little over an hour's drive from Las Vegas, in the moderate-climate of southern Utah, there are numerous places to stay, including some world-class spa and golf resorts. This bed and breakfast is one of two unique places in the area. The thirteen rooms here are all different and one in particular is unusual, with a spa tub for two inside an authentic 1927 Model T Ford. Four rooms have spa tubs and fireplaces, some have canopy beds, all have antique furnishings and pioneer artifacts, and all have private baths, TV/VCR, and phone. A full breakfast is included with your stay.

> 217 N. 100 West, St. George, UT 84770
> 800-600-3737
> www.sevenwivesinn.com
> $–$$$$$

~Green Gate Village Bed & Breakfast Inn

This is a most unusual inn, with sixteen units including some entirely restored pioneer houses, ranging from one-bedroom to four-bedrooms. Or, stay in just one room in one of the larger houses, all beautifully restored and some elegant, with period furnishings and antiques. A pool, outdoor spa and tennis courts are situated in the middle of the grounds, with the houses and a store surrounding them, giving this a true village feel. Breakfast is included and served either in the main house or in your room.

> 76 W. Tabernacle, St. George, UT 84770
> 800-350-6999
> www.greengate.com
> $–$$$$$

Texas

Texas is definitely a big state with mostly a Southwestern flavor, with certain retreats particularly conducive to writers and artists included here.

~Carriage House Inn

This is a two-story Colonial house with hardwood floors and ceramic tile floors, containing five rooms with private baths. The inn provides wonderful accessories, such as alarm clocks, magazines, books, allergy filters, beverages in the rooms, as well as all the usual amenities. It also rates as having one of the top ten country breakfasts of any inn in the country.

> 1110 W. 22-1/2 St., Austin, TX 78704
> 866-472-2333
> www.carriagehouseinn.org
> **$$–$$$**

~The Governor's Inn

A ten-room Victorian built in 1897 with verandas on two floors, this inn was totally refurbished in 1993 with antiques and elegant furnishings, including canopy beds, clawfoot tubs in the private baths, and beautiful oriental rugs. All rooms have cable TV, data ports and voicemail, coffee, robes, hair dryers, and breakfast is included. The two listings below this one (The Brook House and Carrington's Bluff) are run by the same proprietor.

> 611 W. 22nd St., Austin, TX 78705
> 888-397-8677
> www.governorsinnaustin.com
> **$–$$$**

~The Brook House

Six rooms in an old mansion, built in 1922.

> 1900 Rio Grand, Austin, TX 78705
> 800-871-8908
> www.judgeshill.com
> **$$–$$$$**

~Carrington's Bluff

An 1877 English country house, located near the university.

> 1900 David St., Austin, TX 78705
> 888-290-6090
> **$$**

Austin (Lake Travis)
~Lakeway Inn and Resort

About 30 minutes from Austin, this inn is located on one of the prettiest lakes in Texas, and most of the 239 rooms have beautiful lake views. All rooms have high-speed Internet access, data ports, dual phones and voicemail, coffee, air conditioning, room service, satellite TV/HBO, and private baths. This is a large resort with all the recreational activities expected, such as boating, a pool, fitness center, and restaurants, but it is the kind of place one can hole up at, gaze out the window, and work. You can arrange a breakfast-included package.

101 Lakeway Dr., Austin, TX 78734
800-525-3929
www.lakewayinn.com
$$–$$$$$

LOGIC PREVAILS

While authors are unlikely to write a nonfiction book from front to back without using an outline, some try, and end up getting stuck.

I think it is important that the structure is laid out logically at the beginning, or the book won't get done. Start with a solid outline for the skeleton of the book and then fill it in while writing. Once you get an outline down on paper, you might see an area that needs to be expanded, or in another chapter, you may see an area that should not be addressed at all. Or, maybe a certain topic doesn't need its own chapter.

Make sure you confirm major changes with your editor early in the writing process. Then, knock off your easiest chapters first.

Save writing the Introduction for the very last, so you'll have a better understanding of what needs to be included. Then, reorganize the entire outline, if necessary.

If you choose to work at a retreat, get your discipline in place right away. If you drift, it can be dangerous for productivity and, if you have an expansive sense of time, you won't get enough done.

—Deb Werksman, editorial manager of Gift Books at Sourcebooks, Inc.

Comfort
~Meyer Bed & Breakfast on Cypress Creek
This is an 1857 landmark building, featuring nine antique-filled rooms with private baths, a pool, outdoor spa and a hearty breakfast.

845 High St., Meyer, TX 78013
888-995-6100
www.Meyerbedandbreakfast.com
$–$$

Glen Rose
~Cedars on the Brazos B & B
Located on a bluff above the Brazos River, this two-story log bed and breakfast sits on over one-hundred wooded acres. All rooms have private baths, lovely furnishings, porches or decks overlooking the river, and a full breakfast is included. Two suites have writing desks and sitting areas. The inn has a library on the first floor.

2920 County Rd. #413, Glen Rose, TX 76043
254-898-1000
www.cedarsonthebrazos.com
$$–$$$

Fort Worth
~The Ashton
This historic inn was built in 1915, but totally refurbished in 2001 and is on the National Register of Historic Places. The 39 elegant rooms all have spa tubs in the private baths, and include modern features, such as modems, data ports, cable TV, robes, and coffee. Located right in downtown, this inn is a Texas treasure.

610 Main St., Fort Worth, TX 76102
817-332-0100
www.theashton.com
$$$$–$$$$$

Fredericksburg
~Das College Haus Bed & Breakfast
A lovely Victorian in Greek Revival style, this four-room inn dating from 1916, has charming period pieces and antique furnishings throughout. Rooms have private entrances, private baths, coffee, cable TV, hair dryers, and breakfast is included. It's only a short walk to all the quaint shops and restaurants in town.

106 W. College St. Fredericksburg, TX 78624
830-997-9047
www.dascollegehaus.com
$$–$$$

League City

~South Shore Harbour Resort

Just thirty minutes south of Houston on lovely Clear Lake, this resort is easy for Houston residents to escape to when desiring a close encounter with water. It is a large, modern hotel but most of the 250 rooms have fabulous views of the water and marina and, all the amenities necessary, including large, modern, private baths, desks, modem connections, cable TV, room service and a bar/restaurant. There is a tropical pool with waterfall and a fitness center.

2500 S. Shore Harbour Blvd., League City, TX 77575
800-442-5005
www.sshr.com
$$–$$$$$

Mineola

~Fall Farm

This ten-acre country farmhouse is elegant and comfortable and about an hour and a half from both Dallas and Shreveport, Louisiana. There are two rooms, three suites, and a cottage/guest house available, all with private baths, fine linens, and sitting areas to work in. Full breakfast, afternoon refreshments, and wine are included at this serene East Texas location, and there is a pool and spa.

2027 FM. 779, Mineola, TX 75773
877-886-7696
www.fallfarm.com
$$$–$$$$$

San Antonio

~Hotel Valencia Riverwalk

This 213-room hotel was completed in 2002, and is located directly on the famed San Antonio Riverwalk. No expense was spared in creating comfortable, functional, and beautiful rooms, with custom-designed beds, beverages, refrigerators, safes, modem connections, data ports, elegant bathrooms, and 24-hour room service available in five different languages. Breakfast is included in the room price .The twelve-story building is a lovely addition to the waterfront.

150 E. Houston St., San Antonio, TX 78205
210-227-9700
www.hotelvalencia.com
$$–$$$$$

ART THAT PLEASES

I can't emphasize enough that we want to see well-done art samples—especially with realistic art. The sample art must not make you wince, so no crossed eyes and no crooked noses. We can't be forgiving.

Too much art is tired-looking. Art directors are looking for fresh styles. At Viking, artists would say they were the next Lane Smith. Many artists send us samples that do not show children or animals. If you are interested in illustrating picture books, we need to see at least three to four sequential scenes of the same children and/or animals interacting in different settings. These scenes should show the development of a narrative through a variety of moods, situations and settings while maintaining a consistency of style and character. They should use color, scale and composition to convey the pacing of a story. If an artist is interested in jacket assignments, we need to see full color illustrations of figures and portraits in a setting. The specifics of the period, location, style, and mood are critical, since the jacket reveals the distinguishing features of a novel.

We recommend that you visit your library and bookstore to learn more about the style of art the publishers look for. This will be useful in selecting which aspects of your work you wish to show in your portfolio. We review portfolios on Tuesdays but do not make appointments. You can drop off by 11 A.M. and pick up after 4 P.M. If you cannot drop off your portfolio, you can send samples by mail. We prefer printed samples or color copies, and make sure your name, address, and phone number are marked clearly. If you want samples returned, you must send a self-addressed stamped envelope. Do not send original art, slides, or disks or e-mailed samples.

—Cecilia Yung, art director for G.P. Putnam's Sons and Philomel Books, divisions of the PenguinGroup in New York City

~Menger Hotel

Since 1859, this 300-room hotel has been the premiere hotel of San Antonio. Across from the Alamo, this five-story historic hotel has Victorian and contemporary rooms beautifully decorated, with all the amenities of a fine hotel. Some rooms overlook the Alamo or Alamo Plaza, and there is a pool and outdoor spa, as well as a restaurant and bar.

> 204 Alamo Plaza, San Antonio, TX 78205
> 210-223-4361
> www.historicmenger.com
> $$$

~The Oge' Inn on the Riverwalk

Located in the historic district along the Riverwalk on 1.5-beautiful acres, this Antebellum mansion, built in 1857, has ten rooms, all with private baths, TV, phone, refrigerator, and seven have fireplaces and half have porches. Large verandas grace both floors, adding to the elegance of this inn, which serves a complimentary breakfast. Furnished with both American and European antiques, the inn is only several blocks from the Alamo, shopping areas and the convention center.

> 209 Washington St., San Antonio, TX 78204
> 800-242-2770
> www.ogeinn.com
> $$$-$$$$

~Beckmann Inn and Carriage House

This lovely Victorian inn is located in the historic district, across the street from The Riverwalk. The three rooms and two suites are filled with antiques and provide private baths, robes, TV, phone, and refrigerator. Full breakfast is included and served on fine china on the charming wraparound porch.

> 222 E. Guenther St., San Antonio, TX 78204
> 800-945-1449
> www.beckmanninn.com
> $$-$$$

Wimberley
~Blair House

Outside the artists' community of Wimberley, high up in the Texas hill country, is this highly acclaimed inn on 22 acres. The nine rooms, all with private baths, are all luxurious with great attention to every detail and flowers and art are present throughout. Rated as one of the top ten inns in Texas, the inn offers a full breakfast and complimentary wine, as well as an excellent restaurant in the building.

> 100 Spoke Hill Rd., Wimberley, TX 78676
> 877-549-5450
> www.blairhouseinn.com
> $$$–$$$$$

THE
ROCKY MOUNTAIN STATES

Colorado

Wyoming

Montana

South Dakota

Big skies, big mountains, big rivers—the magnificent scenery of the Rockies is perfect for creative types longing for true solitude.

Colorado

Denver

~*Castle Marne Inn*

This mansion, built in 1889, and located in the Wyman historic district of Denver, is on the National Historic Register. The four-story Victorian-style inn was built by William Lang, a famous architect, and features stained glass, a four-story tower and stone and wood throughout. The seven rooms and two suites are all elegant with antique furnishings, private baths (two with spa tubs), and a full breakfast and afternoon tea are included and served in the dining room and parlor. There are English gardens and an outdoor spa.

> 1572 Race St., Denver, CO 80206
> 800-92-MARNE
> www.castlemarne.com
> $$–$$$$$

~*Magnolia Hotel*

Located right in downtown, this elegant, historic, upscale European-style hotel has 244 rooms, including some suites with kitchenettes. Complete business services are available, including high-speed Internet access, and a fitness center and restaurant/bar are located on the premises. Breakfast and an afternoon reception are included in the room rate.

> 818 17th St., Denver, CO 80202
> 888-915-1110
> www.magnoliahotel.com
> $$$–$$$$$

Aspen

~*The Little Nell Hotel*

This 92-room mix of a country inn and elegant hotel sits right under Aspen Mountain. All rooms express total luxury and include fireplaces, TV/VCR, phones, plush chairs or loveseats, and most have balconies with gorgeous mountain views and spa tubs or steam showers. Room service is available, and there is a restaurant, a bar and catering services. Impeccable service and attention to every detail make this a special place.

675 E. Durant St., Aspen, CO 81611
970-920-4600
www.thelittlenell.com
$$$$$

Breckenridge
~Allaire Timbers Inn

Instead of the famous Lodge & Spa at Breckenridge, try this beautiful log bed and breakfast with eight rooms and two suites, all named after Colorado mountains. All rooms have private baths and decks with fabulous views, robes, TV, phone, and luxurious amenities. A full breakfast, afternoon refreshments and desserts are included in the great room with fireplace, attached sunroom and loft, and there is an outdoor spa to highlight the inn's rustic elegance.

9511 Hwy. 9, Box 4653, Breckenridge, CO 80424
800-624-4904
www.allairetimbers.com
$$$–$$$$$

~Great Divide Lodge

This unpretentious inn has 208 spacious and contemporary rooms and may be the perfect choice if you are looking for a simple, comfortable, pretty room with all the basics—private bath, robes, refrigerator, coffee, balconies with mountain views, and lodge amenities, such as a pool, spa, room service, all located only two blocks from Main Street and close to skiing.

550 Village Rd., Breckenridge, CO 80424
888-906-5698
www.greatdividelodge.com
$$–$$$$$

Redstone
~Redstone Inn

Located about three hours from Denver, near Aspen, this historic, hundred-year-old inn has antique Stickley furniture, yet, all the modern conveniences, including a pool and fitness center. There are six rooms, two with a shared bath. Breakfast is included, and the quaint town is known for its arts and crafts, with many artisan studios around.

> 82 Redstone Rd., Redstone, CO
> 800-748-2524
> www.redstoneinn.com
> $–$$$$

Twin Lakes
~Mount Elbert Lodge

A little over 2-hours drive from Denver, near Aspen, you will find some of the most gorgeous mountain views in the state, as you gaze at the 13,000 to 14,000-foot peaks of Mount Elbert, Mount Massive, and Mount Hope. The lodge, which used to be an 1880s roadhouse on the way from Aspen to Denver, is now a charming, yet rustic, inn with five rooms and eight cabins. Open year-round, the rooms are cozy and quaint and decorated in a frontier tradition, with quilts and Victorian art, and two rooms have spa tubs in the private baths. There are two rooms with shared baths. Breakfast is included, as is Saturday supper in the winter. Otherwise, there are no restaurants nearby, so bring food. This is a true mountain escape.

> P.O. Box 40, Twin Lakes, CO 81251
> 800-381-4433
> www.mount-elbert.com
> $–$$$

Durango
~Apple Orchard Inn

A year-round inn, located eight miles from Durango in a beautiful, wooded setting, this inn has four rooms in the main house and six separate fairy tale-like cottages. All rooms have private baths, featherbeds, armoires, and sitting areas and each is uniquely decorated, with country-style furnishings and plush comforters. Some rooms and suites have spa tubs, fireplaces, patios or porches, and some have views of the mountains or ponds. Complimentary breakfast, afternoon refreshments, wine and beer and homemade cookies are included.

7758 County Rd. 203, Durango, CO 81301
800-426-0751
www.appleorchardinn.com
$–$$$$

Mesa Verde: National Park/Monument
~Far View Lodge
From April 1 through October 31, this lodge is open and it has no phones or TVs in the rooms, so it is a quiet, inspiring place for writers and artists. The views of the mesa are amazing, but the rooms are pretty basic motel-like rooms with private baths and balconies, and the deluxe rooms have refrigerators, hair dryers, king beds and upgraded furnishings. There is no room service. Avoid summer when families and children overrun the park.

P.O. Box 277, Mancos, CO 81328
800-449-2288
www.visitmesaverde.com
$$

Crestone
~Crestone Mountain Zen Center
There are two retreats in this gorgeous mountain town that are conducive for writers looking for a place to meditate as well as create. This one is situated on 80 acres, with a meditation dome, organic gardens, and dormitory arrangement but there are plenty of places to write and draw.

P.O. Box 130, Crestone, CO 81131
719-256-4692
www.dharmasangha.com
$

~Nada Monetary–Spiritual Life Institute
Another retreat, but more spiritual, with private rooms.

P.O. Box 219, Crestone, CO 81131
719-256-4778
nada@fone.net
$–$$

Ouray

~China Clipper Inn

Known as the "Switzerland of America," this bed and breakfast has twelve rooms all named after famous clipper ships and many of the individualized rooms have a nautical theme in décor. All rooms have ceiling fans as air conditioning is not necessary at the high elevation of Ouray. The rooms also have private baths, decks, fireplaces and in-room spa tubs. Some rooms have private entrances. Breakfast and afternoon beverages are included, and there is a library and outdoor spa.

> 525 Second St., Ouray, CO 81427
> 800-315-0565
> www.chinaclipperinn.com
> $–$$$

Estes Park

Estes Park is located at the entrance to Rocky Mountain National Park here are several possibilities:

Estes Park

~Streamside Cabins

Located on sixteen well-manicured acres, these one and two-bedroom "cabinsuites" are situated along the Fall River. Some have riverfront rooms, and all have private baths with ceramic tile or marble, carpeting, beamed-cathedral ceilings, alarm clocks. Some suites have spa tubs, fireplaces, full kitchens, cable TV/HBO, patios, gas grills, and two have steam showers. There is local free phone service and an enclosed "swimspa"—one-third is a spa and the rest is a state-of-the-art swim-against-jets area for water aerobics.

> 1260 Fall River Rd., Estes Park, CO 80517
> 800-321-3303
> www.streamsideofestes.com
> $–$$$$

~Timber Creek Chalets

This family-owned resort, with twelve separate cabins, some one-bedroom and some large two-bedroom units. Each chalet is tastefully decorated

Streamside Cabins, Estes Park, CO. Similiar to a small village, this resort lies between Old Man Mountain and the Fall River. Courtesy of Streamside Cabins

and includes modern amenities such as cable TV/HBO, phone, data port, private bath, and a picnic table. Most have fully-equipped kitchens, some with wood-burning fireplaces, and there is an outdoor, heated pool, spa and gas grills.

2115 Fall River Rd., Estes Park, CO 80517
800-347-1212
www.estespark.com/timbercreek
$–$$$$

~Rockmount Cottages

The Fall river runs through this scenic property, which has fifteen cottages and four log cabins. The cottages are a cross between a rustic-looking lodge and a modern hotel, with knotty pine wooden walls and beamed ceilings, but modern kitchens and bathrooms. All units have cable TV, outdoor grills and many have fireplaces and are right on the river. There is no maid service.

1852 State Hwy. 66, Estes Park, CO 80517
970-586-4168
www.rockmountcottages.com
$$–$$$

~Fawn Valley Inn

There are motel units, condominium units, and cottages available here and the river and mountain views from the private decks are spectacular. Rooms have private baths, fireplaces, kitchens, cable TV, and there are some spa tub suites. There is also an outdoor pool and spa, as well as picnic tables.

2760 Fall River Rd., Estes Park, CO 80517
800-525-2961
www.fawnvalleyinn.com
$$$–$$$$

~Taharaa Mountain Lodge

This is a beautiful and luxurious bed and breakfast lodge built of stone and logs in 1997, with magnificent mountain views, set on five wooded acres. There are nine rooms and three suites, and all rooms have private baths, fireplaces, writing desks, and decks, and luxurious amenities. Breakfast is included.

> 3110 S. St. Vrain, Estes Park, CO 80517
> 800-597-0098
> www.taharaa.com
> $$$–$$$$$

Telluride
~The San Sophia Inn

Located in the National Historic District of Telluride, this sixteen-room inn also has ten condominium units available. Rooms are lovely, with brass beds, down comforters, fine linens and quilts, private baths with soaking tubs, TV/VCR and beautiful mountain views from most rooms. A full breakfast and wine and appetizers are included in the room price. It's a short walk to the shops and restaurants in town.

> 330 W. Pacific, Telluride, CO 81435
> 800-537-4781
> www.sansophia.com
> $$–$$$$$

Colorado Springs and Southern Colorado

Colorado Springs
~Holden House Bed & Breakfast Inn

Built in 1902, this Colonial Revival Victorian mansion has five rooms in the main inn, as well as additional rooms in the carriage house—all unique and beautifully decorated with country charm and antique furnishings. All the rooms are spacious with private baths and soaking tubs, fireplaces, air conditioning and sitting areas. One room has a great view of the gardens, one of the mountains, and one has a porch swing on a private veranda. There are computer hook-ups available, fax, phones, 24-hour coffee and cookies, and a full breakfast is included.

> 1102 W. Pikes Peak Ave., Colorado Springs, CO 80904
> 888-565-3980

www.holdenhouse.com
$$–$$$

~Our Hearts Inn

Located in old Colorado City, this Victorian country house was built in 1895 with curved ceilings. The four individualized rooms all have private baths, queen beds, air conditioning, phone, TV/VCR, stereo, fireplace, a spa tub or clawfoot tub, and garden views. One room has white wicker furniture, and another is decorated in Western style, with a kitchenette, and all rooms have custom-stenciled walls, old photos and much nostalgic charm. A full breakfast is included and refreshments are available all day.

2215 W. Colorado Ave., Colorado Springs, CO 80904
800-533-7095
www.ourheartsinn.com
$$–$$$

~Cheyenne Canon Inn

Adjacent to the Cheyenne Canyon Park, this former bordello and casino was built in 1921. Now it is a beautiful and historic bed and breakfast with nine rooms and one suite, all beautifully-decorated, with private baths, fireplaces, TV/VCR, feather pillows, and some rooms have views of the gardens and rock walls on the grounds. A full breakfast, afternoon reception, and outdoor spa are included in the room price.

2030 W. Cheyenne Blvd., Colorado Springs, CO 80906
800-633-0625
www.cheyennecanoninn.com
$$–$$$

~The Broadmoor

This large-scale hotel has to be mentioned as it is the "grande dame of the Rockies," and while the hotel itself is magnificent and the grounds beautiful and soothing, it probably has too many distractions to be recommended for most creative people to hole up in and work. Built in 1891, the structure is elegant, with stone, marble, and everything else one would expect of a four-star, luxury hotel.

One Lake Ave., Colorado Springs, CO 80906
800-634-7711
www.Broadmoor.com
$$–$$$$$

The Broadmoor, Colorado Springs, CO. This legendary hotel has everything from expansive grounds, lakes, mountain views and all kinds of amenities to wonderful restaurants and nooks and crannies perfect to hideout in.
Courtesy of Andrea Brown

Manitou Springs
~Two Sisters Inn

This lovely town is located right next to Colorado Springs, and is situated at the base of Pike's Peak. This small bed and breakfast has four charming Victorian bedrooms, offering either shared or private baths, and a cottage in white wicker with a skylight and fireplace. Originally built in 1919, the inn has stained glass front door, original hardwood floors, and a library. A full breakfast and snacks are included.

10 Otoe Place, Manitou Springs, CO 80829
800-2-SIS-INN

www.twosisinn.com
$–$$

~Rockledge Country Inn

Built in 1912, each of the five rooms in this inn is a full luxury suite, with king-sized featherbeds, sitting areas, beautiful private baths, and some have fireplaces or spa tubs. The "cottage" room has a full kitchen. Breakfast and an afternoon reception are included on this 3.5 acre estate with lovely gardens, mountain views, and stone walks and patio.

328 El Paso Blvd., Manitou Springs, CO 80829
888-685-4515
www.rockledgeinn.com
$$$$–$$$$$

~The Cliff House at Pike's Peak

Built in 1873 along the stage coach line, by 1880, the inn had electricity. In 1990, the inn spent 10 million dollars in renovation to make this Queen Anne Victorian a state-of-the-art hotel, with high-speed Internet access, cable TV/HBO, free movies, and steam showers. There are 55 rooms and suites all elegant and all slightly different, and some have turret ceilings. All rooms have private baths with brass and marble, and some with spa tubs. All rooms have robes, safes, heated toilet seats, voicemail and coffee. Former guests include Clark Gable, Teddy Roosevelt, Henry Ford and Thomas Edison. Continental breakfast is included and the restaurant in the inn is spectacular, as are the views from the veranda of Pike's Peak.

306 Canon Ave., Manitou Springs, CO 80829
888-212-7000
www.Thecliffhouse.com
$$$–$$$$$

Canon City

~St. Cloud Hotel

This unpretentious, yet historic hotel has had two locations, first built in 1883, in the mining town of Silver Cliff, it was then moved brick by brick to Canon City in 1886. Listed on the National Register of Historic Places, this four-story hotel has 35 cozy rooms and suites, with modern amenities, such as a TV, phone, private baths and a restaurant on the main floor next to the lobby, making this a perfect spot to hole up. Located right in the middle of town, there are shops and restaurants steps away.

631 Main St., Canon City, CO 81212
719-276-2000
www.stcloudhotel.com
$–$$

Wyoming

Jackson
~Parkway Inn
In this old west town, near Jackson Hole and national parks, sits this 37-room inn that also offers suites and cottages. Rooms are charming, with private baths and all the basic hotel amenities, including a fitness center, pool, spa, and sauna. Lots of antique furnishings and wood floors and beamed ceilings give this inn a rustic, yet elegant, touch. Breakfast and snacks are included in the room price.

125 Jackson St., Jackson, WY 83001
800-247-8390
www.parkwayinn.com
$$–$$$$

Teton Village
~Alpenhof Lodge
Located near Jackson Hole, this Bavarian inn is charming, with mountains all around, and offers 42 rooms and suites, all with private baths, down comforters and robes. Some rooms contain fireplaces and balconies, and all include an expansive continental breakfast.

P.O. Box 288, Teton Village, WY 83025
800-732-3244
www.alpenhoflodge.com
$$–$$$$$

Yellowstone National Park
~Lake Yellowstone Hotel and Mammoth Hot Springs Hotel

These two wonderful, historic hotels are located in one of the greatest parks in America, however there may be many distractions here. If you are able to stay focused, try one of these gems: The Lake Yellowstone Hotel, built in 1891 and renovated in the 1920s, is on the National Register of Historic Places, and is situated right on Yellowstone Lake. The hotel is open from May to October, and offers both rooms and private cabins. The Mammoth Hot Springs Hotel was built in 1911 and has over fifty rooms.

> P.O. Box 527, Yellowstone National Park, WY 82190
> 307-344-7901
> www.travelyellowstone.com
> $–$$$$$

THERE'S NO PLACE LIKE HOME

I want to know a good place to send my family, so I can just stay home and write!

—Linda Sue Park, Newberry Award winning author of several novels

Centennial
~Mountain View Historic Hotel

Located about six miles from the Snowy Range ski area, this hotel was built in 1907 and still retains its turn-of-the-century charm. Six unique rooms, with private baths, quilts, TV/VCR, and refrigerators, make this a good place to hideaway. The restaurant in the inn serves all meals at an additional cost.

> 2747 Hwy. 130, Centennial, WY 82055
> 888-400-9953
> www.mtnviewhotel.com
> $–$$

Montana

Gardiner
~*Yellowstone Suites Bed & Breakfast*

Located near the north entrance of Yellowstone National Park at Gardiner (the only winter entrance open to cars), this charming three-story stone inn, built in 1904, boasts four rooms, two with private baths and one with a kitchenette. There is an outdoor spa, a covered veranda with rocking chairs, gardens, an extensive library, and a full breakfast is included.

506 4th St., Gardiner, MT 59030
800-948-7937
www.yellowstonesuites.com
$–$$

Flathead Lake

This is the largest freshwater lake west of the Mississippi River.

Lakeside
~*Flathead Lake Suites*

Three gorgeous condominium suites with lakefront views, elegant furnishings, full kitchens, and one-or two-bedroom units are available for three-night minimums. All the essentials are here, but you should bring food.

P.O. Box 768, Lakeside, MT, 59922
800-214-2204
www.angelpoint.com
$$–$$$

Bigfork
~*Flathead Lake Vacation Rentals*

There are both cabins and full homes available here, with lake views, fully-equipped kitchens, linens, lovely furnishings, barbecue grills, decks, and all the essentials. There is also a private dock and sauna on the premises.

18123 E. Lakeshore, Bigfork, MT 59911
406-982-3073

www.flatheadlakevacationrentals.com
$$–$$$$$

Bozeman

~Cottonwood Inn Bed & Breakfast

Located on top of a hill, this lovely country inn has 5 individually deco-
rated rooms with private baths and luxurious amenities in each room. A full
breakfast is served, there is an outdoor spa with gorgeous mountain views,
and the inn is just minutes from downtown Bozeman.

1315 Cottonwood Canyon Rd., Bozeman, MT 59718
406-763-5452
www.cottonwood-inn.com
$–$$$

MOUNTAIN HIGH

Whether it's the Rockies or the Catskills, I always recommend a mountain
retreat for writers. When it's time to lock things down and hone that final draft,
being alone with your work can be very useful and productive. Rent a cabin
with no extra amenities. Yes, you'll need a phone and radio for emergencies,
and water and power for obvious reasons, but otherwise keep it simple. Walks
in the forest, around lakes, or along streams will do wonders for recharging your
mind. And when you get back to your keyboard, you'll have a clearer sense of
purpose and a firmer grasp on what you're trying to accomplish.

—*Mauro DiPreta, executive editor of Morrow imprint, HarperCollins Publishers*

Ennis

~El Western

This is a 27-room log cabin resort in the heart of the Madison River
valley in southwestern Montana. Built in the 1940s, the cabins are spread
out around the property, with an abundance of horses all around. Cabins
have private baths and kitchens.

P.O. Box 487, Ennis, MT 59729
800-831-2773

www.elwestern.com
$–$$$$$

South Dakota

Rapid City

~Audrie's Bed & Breakfast and Abend Haus Cottages

This was the first bed and breakfast in the Black Hills area, and it has won many awards for its hospitality. Guests have a choice of suites or separate cottages. All units have private entrances, baths, patios, spas, cable TV (some have fireplaces), and all include breakfast and free trout fishing on the inn's own creek. There are seven acres of Black Hills setting to enjoy, a gift shop on the premises, and the B & B is only seven miles west of Rapid City.

23029 Thunderhead Falls Rd., Rapid City, SD 57702
605-342-7788
www.audriesbb.com
$$–$$$

~Flying B Ranch Bed & Breakfast

Located on a 3500-acre cattle ranch, this lovely house has three well-appointed suites with private baths, a heated pool, spa, sauna and a full, ranch breakfast is included.

6324 N. Haines, Rapid City, SD 57701
605-342-5324
www.flyingb.com
$$$

Custer

~Custer Mansion Bed & Breakfast

Built in 1891, this Gothic Victorian mansion has five charming rooms with antiques and stained glass. All have private baths, one has a spa tub and all rooms have air conditioning and a full breakfast is served, overlooking the acre of gardens.

35 Centennial Dr., Custer, SD 57730
877-519-4948
www.custermansionbb.com
$–$$

~French Creek Ranch Bed & Breakfast

This secluded ranch setting is only one mile from Custer State Park. There are three spacious suites with tasteful, Western décor, and all rooms come with private baths, TV, sauna, fireplace, billiards, wet bar, tables, and lots of room to roam. Large, hearty breakfasts, snacks, and beverages are all complimentary.

Hwy. 16A East, Box 588, Custer, SD 57730
877-673-4790
$$

Lennox

~Steever House Bed & Breakfast

In the Great Plains of eastern South Dakota, just south of Sioux Falls, sits this charming, Victorian inn with 4 rooms with queen beds, private baths, and a full breakfast and afternoon refreshments are served daily.

46850 276th St., Lennox, SD 57039
605-647-5055
www.steeverhouse.com
$

Deadwood

~The Historic Franklin Hotel

This historic 55-room inn was built in 1903 and some its guests include John Wayne, Willie Nelson, and Kevin Costner. There are also modern rooms .in the motel part of the hotel across the street, but the historic rooms are wonderful, filled with Victorian antiques, and all have private baths. There is a restaurant and gaming is available.

700 Main St., Deadwood, SD 57732
800-688-1876
www.deadwood.net/franklin
$–$$

6

THE
MIDWEST

Minnesota

Wisconsin

Nebraska

Iowa

Michigan

Illinois

Indiana

Ohio

Minnesota

This is the land of endless lakes, so we suggest finding your favorite lake, pack your favorite snacks, and hole up as long as you can.

Afton

~Afton House Inn

Built in 1867, this historic inn, located in the historic town of Afton on the St. Croix River, just east of St. Paul, has twenty-five beautiful and unique rooms with antique furnishings, fireplaces, TV, private baths, and some spa tubs. Deluxe rooms have balconies overlooking the river. A full breakfast is included and the restaurant on the premises is known for its fine cuisine.

> 3291 S. St. Croix Trail, Afton, MN 55001
> 877-436-8883
> www.aftonhouseinn.com
> $–$$$$$

Bemidji

~Beltrami Shores B & B

This Northwoods inn has three individualized rooms constructed of cedar logs, with private baths and decks with views of Beltrami Lake. On eighteen wooded acres, the inn has a lovely sitting room, library, greatroom and porch. A full, hearty breakfast is included.

> 5554 Island View Dr. NE, Bemidji, MN 56601
> 888-746-7373
> www.beltramishores.com
> $–$$

Crane Lake

~Voyagaire Lodge and Houseboats

On the south entrance of Voyageurs National Park, you should try renting a houseboat on Crane Lake. They come in sizes suiting 2-8 people, with fully-equipped kitchens, bathrooms, and all the necessities needed for one night or one week on the water. The houseboats are nicely decorated and comfortable. Or, if you just want a view of the lake, stay at the lodge. The twelve rooms vary from studios to three-bedroom units, and all have private baths, kitchens, decks, and pretty furnishings.

> 7576 Gold Coast Rd., Crane Lake, MN 55725
> 800-882-6287
> www.voyagaire.com
> $–$$$$$

Duluth
~A.G. Thomson House
This historic 1909 bed and breakfast, voted one of the top inns in America, as it has six elegant suites with private baths, spa tubs, air conditioning, fireplaces and beautiful views of Lake Superior. A full breakfast is included at this charming, three-story inn.

> 2617 E. 3rd St. Duluth, MN 55812
> 877-807-8077
> www.thomsonhouse.biz
> $$–$$$$$

~The Cotton Mansion
The mansion features 7 luxurious suites, all with private baths, spa tubs, air conditioning, and attention to every detail. There are wonderful common rooms, such as a library, gallery, dining room, sunroom and porch. A full breakfast is included.

> 2309 E. 1st St., Duluth, MN 55812
> 800-228-1997
> www.bbonline.com/mn/cottonmansion
> $$–$$$.

Lanesboro
~Historic Scanlan House Bed & Breakfast
This Queen Anne Victorian, built in 1889, is one of Minnesota's oldest operating B & Bs. The five rooms and two suites all have air conditioning, private baths, lots of antique furnishings, stained glass, and elaborate wood detailing. The suites also have spa tubs and fireplaces. A five-course breakfast is included in the price.

708 Parkway Ave. S., Lanesboro, MN 55949
800-944-2158
www.scanlanhouse.com
$–$$$$

Lanesboro
~Berwood Hill Inn

This elegant, hillside bed and breakfast has been named to many "best lists," and *Travel & Leisure Magazine* reports, "it's as luxurious as a B&B can get." The three rooms and two suites, with air conditioning, private baths including either spa tubs or clawfoot tubs, are elegant, with antique décor and beautiful views of the valley. Suites have sitting areas and window seats, and there are porches on both floors that overlook the gardens. A five-course breakfast is included.

RR 2, Box 22, Lanesboro, MN 55949
800-803-6748
www.berwood.com
$–$$$$

Little Marais
~Stone Hearth Inn

This four-room inn, dating from the 1920s is located 66 miles north of Duluth, but it is a world away, with breathtaking Lake Superior views—with two rooms located right on the shore. The inn is comfortably furnished and a continental breakfast is included.

6598 Lakeside Estates Rd., Little Marais, MN
888-206-3020
www.stonehearthinn.com
$$–$$$

Little Marais
~Spirit of Gitche Gumee

Don't let the name scare you away from this charming getaway with two of the four rooms boasting wonderful views of Lake Superior. All rooms are cozy and comfortable, with private baths, and a continental breakfast of homemade muffins is included.

Berwood Hill Inn, Lanesboro, MN. Years of work have gone into producing the colorful and immaculate gardens surrounding this charming Victorian inn. Courtesy of Berwood Hill Inn

North shore of Lake Superior.
6228 Hwy. 61, Little Marais, MN 55614
218-226-6476
www.gitchegumee.net
$

Minneapolis
~Elmwood House Bed & Breakfast
This four-room inn is listed on the National Register of Historic Places and it is located in a quiet, residential part of the city. The rooms all have comfortable furnishings, lots of period pieces, private baths, and a full breakfast is included. The common rooms include a lovely living room with fireplace, parlor, and dining room.

One E. Elmwood Pl., Minneapolis, MN 55419
888-822-4558
www.elmwoodhouseus.com
$–$$

New Prague
~Schumacher's Hotel
This inn and restaurant is less than an hour from the Twin Cities and has won awards for its cuisine. The fifteen rooms and one suite all have private baths with spa tubs, fireplaces, and luxurious details, including period furnishings. After enjoying the included breakfast, stroll through the gardens.

212 W. Main St., New Prague, MN 56071
800-283-2049
www.schumachershotel.com
$$$–$$$$$

Red Wing
~St. Hubert House
This is Minnesota's only historic French Gallery-style mansion and it overlooks Lake Pepin, just outside of Red Wing. Located on six acres, the inn

was built in 1855 and has five rooms and three suites that include private baths, soaking tubs, air conditioning, beautiful antique furnishings and a full breakfast is provided. The bottom floor has a screened-in porch, historic library, antiques, and a Steinway grand piano.

29055 Garrard Ave., Old Frontenac, MN 55026
507-452-4045
www.sthuberthouse.com
$$$–$$$$$

GET THE FACTS RIGHT

I am attracted to authors who are well-paired with their subject for personal or professional reasons. I'm most drawn to projects that present a familiar subject freshly or a less well-known subject commercially—incorporating an angle that reaches out to a mass audience. When it comes to writing nonfiction, an author should never lose sight of his reader—imagine what he or she needs and wants to know about the subject.

—Rita Rosenkranz, literary agent, New York

Stillwater

~The Rivertown Inn

Recently renovated, this inn's nine rooms are all named after nineteenth century poets. All the rooms have private baths with spa tubs, fireplaces, individual, elegant furnishings, and luxurious amenities. A full breakfast, afternoon wine, and appetizers are included in the price, and it is a short walk to downtown.

306 W. Olive St., Stillwater, MN 55082
651-430-2955
www.rivertowninn.com
$$$–$$$$$

Wisconsin

There are numerous excellent writers' retreats along the lakes of Wisconsin.

Bailey's Harbor
~*Blacksmith Inn*
This inn offers fifteen cottage rooms with fabulous views of the harbor from private balconies. All rooms have private baths with spa tubs, fireplaces, air conditioning, TV, and elegantly rustic décor. There is a private beach, and a continental breakfast is served on the porch overlooking the water.

> 8152 Hwy. 57, Bailey's Harbor, WI 54202
> 800-769-8619
> www.theblacksmithinn.com
> $$–$$$$

Bayfield
~*Old Rittenhouse Inn*
This glorious location on Lake Superior offers two houses with fourteen rooms, three suites, and a cottage. The rooms are beautifully appointed, with antique furnishings in the Queen Anne Victorian style, and include fireplaces, spa tubs, and luxurious amenities. All the rooms have private baths, wonderful lake views, and a full breakfast is included. On many weekends, there are special events, so weekdays may be the best time to visit this inn.

> 301 Rittenhouse Ave., Bayfield, WI 54814
> 888-560-4667
> www.rittenhouseinn.com
> $$–$$$$$

Cable
~*Garmisch Resort*
Located on Lake Namakagon, this historic, rustic inn is surrounded by forests, and most rooms offer lovely lake views. The lodge itself has twelve rooms, but there are also vacation homes available. The inn was handcrafted in the 1920s and there are still elegant touches, as well as wildlife mounts

throughout the lodge. All rooms have private baths, TV, phone, fireplace, and some have decks. The inn is closed from March until May 1.

HC73, Cable, WI 54821
800-794-2204
www.garmischresort.com
$–$$$$$

IDEAS ARE EVERYWHERE

Make your manuscript portable by placing it in a binder. And, carry it around with you—always. It is hard to put some time aside to write. With the binder under your arm, the project will be constantly active in your mind. As you walk on the beach or see a film, you will be searching for relevant ideas, stories, quotations and sources.

—*from* Successful NonFiction *by Dan Poynter, author and publisher*

Egg Harbor
~Door County Lighthouse Inn B&B

A lighthouse tower tops this charming inn, and the five rooms are all decorated inn a nautical style, and all have private baths, air conditioning, TV/VCR, and decks and some have fireplaces and spa tubs. A full breakfast is included and lighthouse tours are available.

4639 Orchard Rd., Egg Harbor, WI 54209
920-868-9088
www.dclighthouseinn.com
$$–$$$$

Gills Rock
~Harbor House Inn

The five rooms at this charming inn, located on a bluff overlooking the quaint fishing harbor, all have decks, private baths, TV, refrigerators, and microwaves. Located only a short walk to the ferry to the islands, there is also an outdoor spa and a sauna, and breakfast is included.

12666 Hwy. 42, Gills Rock, WI 54210
920-854-5196
www.door-county-inn.com
$–$$$$

Green Lake
~Heidel House Resort

Located on beautiful Green Lake, this large resort hotel has many distractions, such as golf, pools, fitness centers, and boating, but it is also charming, with beautiful, soothing views and rooms comfortable enough to hole up in, ignoring all the distractions outside. There are four buildings on the estate, with many kinds of room and suite choices available, but all have the amenities of a distinguished, old hotel, which has two restaurants and provides room service.

643 Illinois Ave., Green Lake, WI 54941
800-444-2812
www.heidelhouse.com
$–$$$$$

Madison
~Mansion Hill Inn

Located in the Historic District of this college town and one block from Lake Mendota, this Romanesque Revival structure dates from 1858 and offers eleven magnificent rooms, some with hand-carved marble fireplaces, arched windows, spa tubs or steam showers in private baths, and elegant detailing throughout. There are beautiful antique furnishings, and a large, continental breakfast and beverages are included in the room price.

424 N. Pinckney St., Madison, WI 53703
800-798-9070
www.mansionhillinn.com
$$–$$$$$

Sturgeon Bay
~Along the Beach Bed & Breakfast

The only bed and breakfast located right on Lake Michigan, there are only two rooms here, but both have wonderful water views. One is a two-bedroom unit, and both have air conditioning, cable TV/VCR, hair dryers and there is a private beach nearby. A full breakfast is included.

> 3122 Lake Forest Park Rd., Sturgeon Bay, WI 54235
> 920-746-0476
> www.doorcounty.com
> $$–$$$

~White Lace Inn

Four beautiful Victorian buildings with white picket fences encompass this eighteen-room complex. Rooms are romantic and charming, and include down comforters, quilts, antique period furnishings, TV/VCR, phone, and most rooms here have fireplaces and spa tubs in the private baths. The gardens are elegant and a full breakfast, beverages, and cookies are included in the room price.

> 16 N. 5th Ave., Sturgeon Bay, WI 54235
> 877-948-5223
> www.whitelaceinn.com
> $–$$$$$

Nebraska

Crawford

~High Plains Homestead

This historic inn is famous as the "home of the Drifter Cookshack," and the food is great. There are also two frontier like rooms that are cozy, and peace and quiet exists for miles around.

> 263 Sandcreek Rd., Crawford, NE 69339
> 308-665-2592
> www.highplainshomestead.com
> $

Scottsbluff

~The Candlelight Inn

This is basically a motel, with clean and comfortable rooms, TV/HBO, private baths, and there is a pool, restaurant, and lounge with nice, open views. A continental breakfast included.

> East Hwy. 26, Scottsbluff, NE 69361
> 800-424-2305
> www.candlelightscottsbluff.com
> $

Iowa

Bentonsport
~Mason House Inn
This town is one of Van Buren County's first settlements and Mark Twain lived around here in the 1850s. This area is rustic and secluded, and the inn is a beautiful brick, mansion, built in 1846 by Mormon craftsmen for steamboat travelers. The eight rooms and one cottage all have private baths, air conditioning, and antique furnishings. The cottage also has a refrigerator, microwave, and an upstairs loft, with a view of the Des Moines River. A complimentary breakfast and beverages are included.

> 21982 Hawk Dr., Bentonsport, IA 52565
> 800-593-3133
> www.masonhouseinn.com
> $–$$

Dubuque
~Redstone Inn
This historic town on the upper Mississippi is charming. This inn has fourteen well-appointed rooms, all with private baths, air conditioning, and breakfast is included.

> 504 Bluff St., Dubuque, IA 52001
> 563-582-1894
> www.theredstoneinn.com
> $–$$

~Lighthouse Valleyview Bed & Breakfast
This is an old, historic inn with romantic, antique furnishings throughout and rooms with private baths.

15937 Lore Mound Rd., Dubuque, IA 52002
800-407-7023
www.lighthousevalleyview.com
$–$$$

WHY NOT HIDEOUT IN IOWA

An easy day's drive from nearly every Midwestern city, Iowa is the perfect writer's getaway haven. To the geographically ungrounded, a group that now includes exactly 98.2 percent of all Americans, Iowa is often confused with Ohio and Idaho. One nice aspect about using Iowa as a writing hideout is that it is highly unlikely that anyone who is attempting to suck you into mundane distractions will ever even dream where you've gone off to.

Iowa is bounded by America's two largest rivers, the Mississippi on the east and the Missouri on the west. That fact, plus the huge weight of Minnesota pressing down upon it from the north and Missouri thrusting up from the south, make Iowa nearly a square-shaped state. However, despite its rustic image, the shape of the state is the only thing that is "square" about it. In fact, Iowa has the highest per capita literacy rate in the nation. This makes for nearly 2.5 million potential readers of any given book.

The interior of Iowa is made up of perfectly flat, seemingly endless plains on the western ranges and undulating hills on the eastern stretches. The state resounds with Dutch, German and Scandanavian accents, culture and crafts. Amish and Mennonite communities flourish throughout the state. The backroads are filled with charming villages, bordered by small rivers, creeks, streams and woodlands. One is encouraged by nature to put in a line and recline over a good book or an unfinished manuscript.

—David Marion, *author, editor, and Iowa native*

Maquoketa
~Squiers Manor Bed & Breakfast
Built in 1882, this brick Queen Anne Victorian is situated in a quaint

village along the Grant Wood Scenic Byway. There are eight rooms with private baths, including spa tubs and antique décor. The single suite also has a refrigerator, wood-burning stove, and a reading/writing nook. Breakfast and a candlelit dessert reception in the evening are included.

> 418 W. Pleasant St., Maquoketa, IA 52060
> 563-652-6961
> www.squiersmanor.com
> $–$$$$

Newton
~LaCorsette Maison Inn
This elegant mansion, built in 1909, located just east of Des Moines and close to Grinnell College, which has a terrific library, is on the National Historic Register and its well-appointed rooms all have private baths and quaint details. There are five rooms, with two suites, and all include a French-style breakfast. There are lovely sitting areas and the porch is filled with comfortable white wicker furniture.

> 629 1st Ave., Newton, IA 50208
> 641-792-6833
> $–$$$$

Michigan

Mackinac Island
There are many wonderful places to stay at this charming resort island and we can only list a few, but remember that summer is busy with tourists.

~Metivier Inn
This 21-room country inn was built in 1877. All rooms are beautifully decorated with antique furnishings, have private baths, and there are gardens, porches, and a continental breakfast is included.

> P.O. Box 285, Mackinac Island, MI 49757
> 906-847-6234

www.metivierinn.com
$–$$$$$

~Haan's 1830 Inn

This magnificent Greek Revival-style building has six rooms, all individually decorated with antique furnishings. Breakfast is included.

P.O. Box 123, Mackinac Island, MI 49756
906-847-6244
www.mackinac.com/haans
$$–$$$

~Hotel Iroquois

This historic inn, with 46 flower-themed rooms, is located right in town on the waterfront of Lake Michigan. All rooms and suites have private baths and all luxurious necessities are included. The restaurant serves all meals.

Hotel Iroquois, Mackinac Island, MI 49756
906-847-3321
www.iroquoishotel.com
$$$–$$$$

~Chippewa Hotel

Located right on Main Street, this hotel is situated directly on the water, with many rooms offering beautiful lake views from balconies. All rooms have private baths and include the usual comforts of a nice hotel. The restaurant serves all meals, and affords lovely views.

P.O. Box 250, Mackinac Island, MI 49757
800-241-3341
www.chippewahotel.net
$$–$$$$$

Brooklyn
~Chicago Street Inn B&B

Located in the quaint town of Brooklyn, about an hour from all the major Michigan cities, this charming inn has three rooms in the main house and an available, 1920s bungalow that has a kitchenette, spa tub, and fireplace. The rooms all have private baths and air conditioning. A full breakfast is included.

> 219 Chicago St., Brooklyn, MI 49230
> 517-592-3888
> www.chicagostreetinn.com
> $–$$$

Petoskey
~Stafford's Bay View Inn
Located on the shores of Lake Michigan, in Petoskey's historic district, this charming, Victorian three-story inn has 21 rooms and 9 suites. All the rooms have private baths and the suites have spa tubs. All are elegantly-appointed with antique furnishings. Breakfast is included and a highly-rated restaurant is located in the inn.

> 2011 Woodland Ave., Petoskey, MI 49770
> 800-258-1886
> www.bayviewinn.cm
> $–$$$$$

Lansing/Eaton Rapids
~The English Inn
This stately, Tudor mansion was formerly an automobile baron's residence and now it offers ten rooms looking out at the Grand River, over fifteen acres of gardens, trails, and hillside. The six rooms in the main building, which has a library and a pub, are all handsome and have private baths. There is also a cottage with three bedrooms, a pool, and a fireplace. The restaurant on the premises serves all meals.

> 677 S. Michigan Rd., Lansing/Eaton Rapids, MI 48827
> 517-663-2500
> www.englishinn.com
> $–$$$$

Illinois

Chicago

~Burnham Hotel

This landmark, historic building, constructed in 1895 as the first office building in Chicago, is now a magnificent, boutique hotel on Chicago's Loop, with 103 rooms and 19 suites. All the rooms have private baths, luxury items, gold-and-blue fine fabrics, mahogany writing desks, high-speed Internet access, data ports, dual voice mail phones, robes, and pets are allowed. Suites have spa tubs. Room service is available and a fine restaurant exists on the premises, as well as many shops and restaurants, which are only steps away.

> 1 W. Washington St., Chicago, IL 60601
> 877-294-9712
> www.burnhamhotel.com
> $$$–$$$$$

~Hotel Inter-Continental

In the heart of downtown, this large chain hotel is special because of its indoor pool, surrounded by lavish, gold-and-blue tile and this is where Johnny Weissmuller trained for the Olympics. The rooms are well-appointed, as all the Inter-Continental hotels, although, the rooms are a little on the small side, but all have desks and complete business services.

> 505 N. Michigan Ave., Chicago, IL 60611
> 312-944-4100
> www.ichotelsgroup.com
> $$$$–$$$$$

~Lenox Suites Hotel

Located right off the "Magnificent Mile," this unpretentious, remodeled hotel offeres suites with private baths, kitchens, and sitting areas, and some have two-bedrooms. This hotel offers nothing fancy, but some rooms have park views, and they all have the basic hotel amenities, newspaper, and a fitness center and café on the first floor, and a continental breakfast and is included. This is a good bargain for this neighborhood.

616 N. Rush St., Chicago, IL 60611
800-44-LENOX, 312-337-1000
www.luxenhotels.com
$$–$$$$

~Windy City Inn

Located in residential Lincoln Park on a quiet street sits, this 1886 brick mansion has five rooms in the main house and three available for extended stays in the coach house. All have private baths and individualized, quaint furnishings, and the larger rooms/suites have spa tubs, fireplaces, and writing desks. There is a literary theme at this "urban inn," and one lovely room is called the "Carl Sandburg" room, and the common room downstairs with reading materials and refreshments is called the "Ernest Hemingway Common room." Breakfast is included, there are lovely gardens, and the inn is only a few miles from downtown.

607 W. Deming Pl., Chicago, IL 60614
877-897-7091
www.windycityinn.com
$$–$$$$$

Galena

~Goldmoor Inn

On a bluff overlooking the banks of the Mississippi River, this contemporary country inn has rooms, suites, cottages, and cabins, and all are decorated and equipped with luxurious, modern amenities like satellite TV, modem hook ups, and high-speed Internet access, and all have private, elegant baths. Some of the suites contain fireplaces and spa tubs overlooking the river. A complimentary full breakfast is served, as well as cookies and refreshments throughout the day. Historic Dubuque, Iowa is about 20 minutes away.

9001 San Hill Rd., Galena, IL 61036
800-255-3925
www.goldenmoor.com
$$–$$$$$

~Eagle Ridge Inn & Resort

Only six miles from the quaint, historic town of Galena and 65 miles west of Rockford, this large hotel sits on 6800 acres, including a golf course, and has excellent business services available including modem lines, fax service, room service as well as a fitness center, pool and all the basic large hotel amenities. Some rooms have fireplaces and patios.

444 Eagle Ridge Dr., Galena, IL 61036
800-892-2269
www.eagleridge.com
$$$$–$$$$$

Indiana

These inns are a short drive from Chicago and northern Indiana.

Goshen
~*The Checkerberry Inn*
This Georgian style inn has eleven rooms and three suites and has been rated one of the best inns in the Midwest. Situated on 100 acres of wooded land, this elegant inn has individualized, charming rooms, all with private baths, air conditioning, and luxurious amenities. Breakfast is included and the renowned restaurant also serves dinners nightly.

62644 County Rd. 37, Goshen, IN 46528
574-642-4445
www.checkerberryinn.com
$$–$$$$$

South Bend
~*The Oliver Inn*
Located near the University of Notre Dame, this Victorian inn has nine quaint rooms—all are different, with private baths, air conditioning, cable TV, phones, and some have spa tubs and fireplaces. There is a beautiful library downstairs where a candlelit breakfast is served and included in the room price. Complimentary refreshments are also available.

630 W. Washington St., South Bend, IN 46601
574-232-4545

www.oliverinn.com
$–$$$

~Cushing Manor Inn (formerly Book Inn)

This literary bed and breakfast has five beautifully decorated rooms with antique furnishings and names such as "Jane Austen Room," and "Louisa May Alcott Room," with lots of books abounding. There is air conditioning, phones, private baths and TV, and full breakfast is served, as well as fine teas in the sitting room made of butternut wood.

508 W. Washington St., South Bend, IN 46601
574-288-1990
www.cushingmanorinn.com
$$–$$$

New Harmony

~New Harmony Inn

Established in 1814, this historic town began as a communal place for scientists and scholars and now has over 800 residents, and this inn is a charming and historic old building. Besides comfortable rooms with private baths, there is a wonderful restaurant on the premises.

504 North St., New Harmony, IN 47631
800-782-8605
www.newharmonyinn.com
$–$$$

Ohio

Cincinnati

~Garfield Suites Hotel

This all-suite downtown hotel has spacious and elegant contemporary furnishings, and all suites have living rooms, kitchens, dining areas, private baths, and voicemail and data ports are available. Some of the 150 suites have balconies and all include an expanded continental breakfast. There is a fitness room and one duplex penthouse is available.

2 Garfield Place, Cincinnati, OH 45202
513-421-3355
www.garfieldsuiteshotel.com
$$$–$$$$$

Columbus
~Thurber House

Columbus is the home of Ohio State University and was the home of author/artist, James Thurber during his college years. This building is on the National Register of Historic Places and besides being a museum, bookstore, and classroom facility, the Thurber House offers residency programs for writers. Since 1984, more than forty writers from across the nation have spent some time writing and living in the furnished third-floor apartment where Thurber lived while in Columbus. Acceptance into the residency program is by application only. Usually a stipend is included, and the house is in a quiet, historic neighborhood with lovely gardens around it.

77 Jefferson Ave., Columbus, OH 43215
614-464-1032
www.thurberhouse.org
FOR RESIDENCY PROGRAM STUDENTS ONLY

~The Westin Hotel

Located near by the city center, this Westin is an architectural historical landmark and is listed in the National Historic Registry as having been a hotel for over one-hundred years. The European-style skylights and high ceilings with chandeliers and period furnishings in the lobby make this a grand hotel. The 196 rooms are all modern, and have private baths, with marble and cherrywood furnishings, 24-hour room service and all business services are available, including high-speed Internet access. There is a fitness center and two restaurants/lounge. This is not your typical chain hotel.

310 S. High St., Columbus, OH 43215
800-WESTIN-1, 614-228-3800
www.greatsouthernhotel.com or www.westin.com
$$$–$$$$$

Danville
~The White Oak Inn

Located just north of Columbus, in Amish country, this white-clapboard farmhouse has ten rooms, all with private baths (one with a spa tub). All are decorated beautifully with antique furnishings and three have fireplaces. There are quilts and a porch with rocking chairs, and breakfast is included.

> 29683 Walhonding Rd., Danville, OH 43014
> 740-599-6107
> www.whiteoakinn.com
> $–$$$

Dellroy
~Atwood Lake Resort

This hotel has 104 newly renovated rooms, all with private baths, as well as 17 cottages along Atwood Lake with wonderful views. Most rooms and cottages have private balconies, and the pine-wooded cottages have kitchens and fireplaces and special weekly rates.

> 2650 Lodge Rd., Dellroy, OH 44620
> 800-362-6406
> www.atwoodlakeresort.com
> $$–$$$

Logan
~The Inn at Cedar Falls

Located next to the beautiful Hocking Hills State Park, this restored, yet rustic log cabin inn has nine rooms, as well as separate cottages and cabins. Situated on 75 acres, room choices range from those with showers to spa tubs for two, from writing desks to sitting areas, and there are cabins with fully-equipped kitchens. There is an open kitchen/dining room where the chef creates all meals for groups, retreats, and guests.

> 21190 State Rd. 374, Logan, OH 43138
> 800-653-2557
> www.innatcedarfalls.com
> $–$$$$$

Loudonville
~Little Brown Inn
Writer Louis Bromfield called Loudonville, "the edge of paradise, half-way between Cleveland and Columbus." And if your publisher happens to be Little Brown & Company this is the place for you. This inn has twenty rooms with private baths, all comfortably furnished with TV, air conditioning, phones, and business services, at reasonable weekly rates.

> 940 S. Market St., Loudonville, OH 44842
> 888-994-5525
> $–$$

~The Blackfork Inn
This charming bed and breakfast was built in 1865 and has suites filled with antique furnishings, private baths, and all the basic amenities.

> 303 N. Water St., Loudonville, OH 44842
> 419-994-3252
> www.blackforkinn.com
> $$–$$$

Marietta
~Lafayette Hotel
This small, historic downstown hotel, is on the National Registry of Historic Buildings and most of the 77 rooms overlook the Ohio and Muskingum rivers. The rooms are all comfortably furnished with private baths, cable TV, and room service, and business services are available. Shops and restaurants are located nearby.

> 101 Front St., Marietta, OH 45750
> 800-331-9336
> www.Lafayettehotel.com
> $–$$$$

Rockbridge
~Glenlaurel Inn
Located in the Hocking Hills area of southeastern Ohio, this estate is situated on 140 acres of rolling hills. The Scottish-style country inn has rooms,

suites, cottages, and "crofts." Many of the rooms overlook the Camusfearna Gorge. Rooms in the carriage house, crofts and "Hamlet" cottages have kitchens, spa tubs, fireplaces and decks. All have private baths and well-appointed furnishings. Guests have choices for breakfast and dinners are available.

14940 Mount Olive Rd., Rockbridge, OH 43149
800-809-7378
www.glenlaurel.com
$$–$$$$$

Sugarcreek
~Swiss Village Inn

This town, in Ohio's Amish country, also called "Little Switzerland" is charming with many quaint shops and restaurants. This inn has 16 rooms and one Victorian railroad car you can sleep in, as well. The comfortable parlor room has books, games and refreshments and a complimentary continental breakfast is served here. Each of the rooms has private bath, air conditioning, and some have brass beds and Amish quilts.

206 S. Factory St., Sugarcreek, OH 44681
800-792-6822
www.swissvillageinn.com
$–$$

~Bed & Breakfast Barn Inn & Cabins

This charming, barn-like inn has twelve rooms, all with private baths and some quaint log cabins that have private spa tubs and fireplaces. A full country breakfast is included and a restaurant is located on the premises.

560 Sugarcreek St., Sugarcreek, OH 44681
888-334-2436
$–$$

West Union
~Murphin Ridge Inn

Located in southern Ohio, this 142-acre inn has been named as one of the top inns in the country. There are ten rooms and separate cabins with spa tubs and fireplaces. Many rooms have individual porches, and all have private baths and country-style antique furnishings. The main farmhouse, built in 1828, has three dining rooms with an excellent chef serving all meals to guests and locals, as well as an art gallery.

750 Murphin Ridge Rd., West Union, OH 45693
937-544-2263
www.murphinridgeinn.com
$$–$$$$

THE
HEARTLAND

Oklahoma

Kansas

Missouri

Arkansas

Kentucky

Tennessee

West Virginia

The heartland of our great country has a little bit of everything—lakes, rivers, hills, prairie, endless fields, and wide-open vistas everywhere for inspiration.

Oklahoma

Bartlesville
~*Inn at Price Tower*
Only 45 miles from Tulsa, this one-of-a-kind, spectacular hotel was designed and built by Frank Lloyd Wright. It is the only skyscraper Wright created and contains an arts center, shops, restaurants, galleries, and a museum. Actually, guests sleep in the museum, as the 21 rooms/suites on the top six floors of the museum/building make up the hotel portion. This boutique inn is high-design and contains all the modern amenities one would expect in a luxury hotel, including air conditioning, alarm clocks, safes, refrigerators, cable TV, data ports, phones and private, elegant baths. All the suites are spacious but the Tower suites are two-story, wrap around glass units with astounding prairie views. There is a complimentary continental breakfast and admission to the galleries are included in the room price.

> 510 Dewey Ave., Bartlesville, OK 74003
> 877-424-2424
> www.pricetower.org
> $$–$$$$

Tulsa
~*Central Inn (Howard Johnson Inn)*
Although a chain hotel, this is a "gold medal property" and has been newly remodeled with 81 clean and comfortable rooms with private baths. There is cable TV/HBO, outdoor pool, business services, complimentary continental breakfast and newspaper, and mini-suites with microwaves and refrigerators. The inn is close to downtown and the universities.

> 4724 S. Yale, Tulsa, OK 74135
> 800-446-4656
> $

Kansas

Lawrence
~Circle S Ranch

Located less than an hour west of Kansas City, this twelve-room country inn sits on 1200 acres and has been owned by the same family since the 1860s. The inn has won numerous awards as one of the best and most romantic bed and breakfasts in the country, with its warm, soothing, individualized décor, private baths (some with spa tubs), sitting and writing areas, phones, fireplaces, robes, and other elegant amenities. Rooms have panoramic prairie views. A hearty breakfast and afternoon refreshments are complimentary. There are twelve miles of hiking paths and historic sites are located nearby.

3325 Circle S. Lane, Lawrence, KS 66044
800-625-2839
www.circlesranch.com
$$$–$$$$

Missouri

Boonville
~Four Oaks Farm

Built in the 1880s, this two-story Victorian farmhouse sits on 40 acres of a working farm with views of the countryside. The two guest rooms are decorated with antiques with natural woods and have private baths. Besides a hearty breakfast with eggs provided by the chickens on the farm, there is overnight horse boarding available.

22045 Boonville Rd., Boonville, MO 65233
660-882-8048
$

Independence
~Serendipity Bed and Breakfast

This is Harry Truman country, and the six suites at this Victorian brick mansion, built in 1887, are named for his family and historical Missouri themes. Surrounded by flowers and fountains, the inn has common rooms with Victorian children's books and toys, antique collections, and the side porch has benches, a swing and a hammock. All rooms have private baths, lace curtains, TV, one has a kitchenette, and some have sitting areas. Breakfast is included. Pets are allowed.

116 S. Pleasant St., Independence, MO 64050
800-203-4299
$–$$

IF NOT YOU, WHO?

Have the confidence in yourself to invest in your writing career (yes, career, not hobby!).

Think of it as a financial investment—hey, you could lose it all in the stock market in a flash anyway. That might mean taking a few dollars out of that special fund so you can totally get away and immerse yourself in both the splendor of the place and in your writing. It could be a cottage on the beach in Baja or the Bahamas or right smack in the center of things—Paris or New York City.

Low on funds? Find a library with rich oak shelves or a museum where they let you sit for hours inspired by the works of wonder. Or a botanical garden or a park. Find any place that offers enforced quiet and solitude.

Okay, so you really can't get away. Then create a special room or an area just for your writing and creative efforts. It could be an office equipped with just the right desk, chair, lighting, and computer. Treat it like a business office where you go to work—9 to 5 with a lunch break!

Or do the reverse. Create a quiet haven in a corner behind a splendid Japanese screen where you burn candles and listen to music that inspires. But no matter what, put up a "Do Not Disturb" notice and enforce it! (I love the W Hotel's notice: "Go Away! Please.")

So, there are no excuses of time or money. Do whatever ignites that creative spark! Commit to your writing career. If you won't, who will?

—*Diane Gedymin, editor at i universe, and former editor at HarperCollins.*

Kansas City
~Southmoreland

This Colonial Revival, built in 1913, is located right in the heart of Country Club Plaza, with shops and restaurants just steps away. There are twelve well-appointed, individualized rooms, with private baths and one carriage house suite. Some rooms have fireplaces, spa tubs, or decks, and there are modern business services available, such as modem hookups, fax machines, copiers, etc. Complimentary breakfast and afternoon wine and appetizers are served in the lovely courtyard.

116 E. 46th St., Kansas City, MO 64112
816-531-7979
www.southmoreland.com
$$–$$$$

St. Louis
~Lodge at Grant's Trail By Orlando's

This unusual rustic, yet warm and elegant inn is a bed and breakfast located at the head of Grant's Trail by Orlando Gardens, with stone fireplaces and a Western theme. Rooms are comfortably furnished with private baths.

4398 Hoffmeister Ave., St. Louis, MO 63125
866-314-7829
www.lodgeatgrantstrail.com
$–$$

Arkansas

"There are lots of places here where a writer can find procrastination. In fact, one could develop it to a fine art form here." —Robert Wahl, Arkansan author/illustrator. Wahl is correct about this area as the scenic mountains and lakes in this Ozark region are known to cause bouts of daydreaming so you will have to work hard to stay focused here.

Mountain Home
~Carlton Resort

In the Ozarks near the Missouri border, there are a number of lakes perfect for fishing, boating, or creating great works while gazing at the placid waters and mountains. This resort, recently under new owners, has cabin rooms, cottages, and suites, but only the cabins have decks and lake views. The "Hemingway House" is a four-bedroom unit. All rooms are rustic but comfortable, some units have kitchenettes, and the pool has a lake view.

> 1527 Cranfield Rd., Mountain Home, AR 72653
> 888-377-9496
> www.carltonresort.com
> $–$$$$

~Creekside Cabins

Surrounded by 80 acres of woods, with a running creek, these cabins are all wood, inside and out, with modern amenities such as fully-equipped kitchens, separate bedrooms, private baths with spa tubs, air conditioning, VCR, phone, and grills on the decks.

> 705 Creekside Dr., Norfolk, AR
> Mailing Address: 114 Robinson Loop, Mountain Home, AR 72658
> 870-492-7030
> www.Norfolk.com/creekside
> $–$$

~Mockingbird Bay Resort

Located by Lake Norfolk, these knotty pine cabins are uniquely decorated and all have private baths, kitchens, decks with lake views, air conditioning, cable TV, and skylights. There is a pool and game room on the landscaped grounds and special weekly rates are offered.

> 217 Sycamore Springs Circle, Mountain Home, AR 72653
> 800-831-4151
> www.mockingbirdbayresort.com
> $–$$$

Gamaliel
~Take It Easy Resort

Located on Lake Norfolk, close to Missouri and two hours from Branson, these exceptionally bright and cheery cottages are equipped with one-to three-bedrooms, cable TV, air conditioning, screened porches, picnic tables, all cooking utensils in kitchens, private baths, pretty furnishings such as antiques and quilts, and some have fireplaces. Boat slips are available.

168 CR 812, Gamaliel, AR 72537
870-467-5284
www.Norfolk.com/takeiteasy
$–$$

Little Rock
~Peabody Little Rock Hotel
Located above the conference center and the Arkansas River, this luxury hotel has over 400 modern rooms with every luxurious amenity, including data ports and high-speed Internet access. There is a fitness center, a complimentary breakfast and an evening reception is included, and 24-hour room service is available. One of the three hotel restaurants is "Josephine's Library."

3 Statehouse Plaza, Little Rock, AR 72201
800-732-2639
www.peabodylittlerock.com
$$–$$$

~The Empress of Little Rock
This historic and elegant bed and breakfast boasts five rooms and three suites, all furnished with antiques and with luxurious details in each room. The staircase has a stained-glass skylight above, and a full breakfast is served by candlelight. All rooms have private baths, fireplaces, robes, data ports, and cable TV.

2120 Louisiana St., Little Rock, AR 72206
877-374-7966
www.theempress.com
$$–$$$$

Kentucky

Burlington

~Willis Graves Bed and Breakfast

Located in Northern Kentucky, only about 30 minutes from Cincinnati, but a world away from the roar of the city, this lovely inn, built in 1833 by a county clerk named Willis Graves. There are five antique-furnished rooms with private baths, big, fluffy feather pillows, quilts, and high-speed Internet access. A full breakfast is included and historic sites such as the Dinsmore Homestead are nearby.

> 5825 N. Jefferson St. Burlington, KY 41005
> 888-226-5096
> www.burligrave.com
> $–$$$

Corbin

~Dupont Lodge

Located at Cumberland Falls State Resort Park, part of the Daniel Boone National Forest, this 52-room inn is rustic with its stone fireplaces and hemlock and knotty pine beams and paneling, but it has all the necessary amenities and wonderful views. Adjacent to the lodge there are private cottages available with daily maid service, and some have kitchens and fireplaces.

> 7351 Hwy. 90, Corbin, KY 40701
> 800-325-0063
> www.cumberlandfallspark.com
> $–$$$

Harrodsburg

~Beaumont Inn

This historic country inn built in 1845, is found in central Kentucky Bluegrass country, just 32 miles southwest of Lexington. The grand Southern mansion has 33 one-bedroom suites, all with private baths and luxurious amenities. A hearty, full breakfast is included in the room price.

638 Beaumont Inn Dr., Harrodsburg, KY 40330
800-352-3992
www.beaumontinn.com
$–$$$$

Lexington
~The Gratz Park Inn
This historic, charming, small hotel located in a perfectly southern set-
ting, has 38 one-bedroom rooms, four suites with sitting rooms, and two
VIP suites with additional studies. All rooms/suites have private baths, data
ports, phones, cable TV, and include a complimentary breakfast. There are
special weekly rates and meal plans available.

120 W. Second St., Lexington, KY 40507
800-752-4166
www.gratzparkinn.com
$$$–$$$$$

~The Springs Inn
Welcoming guests since 1848, this beautiful Colonial inn has lovely gardens, an outdoor-heated pool, gift shop, and fitness room. The well-appointed
rooms have private baths, alarm clocks, data ports, air conditioning, and a
continental breakfast is included.

2020 Harrodsburg Rd., Lexington, KY 40503
800-354-9503
www.springsinn.com
$$$–$$$$

Tennessee

Kingston
~Whitestone Inn
This elegant country inn is located right on Watts Bar Lake, amid the
Smoky Mountains. There are twenty rooms and suites with bird themes,
and all have fireplaces, private baths with spa tubs, refrigerators, and TV/

VCR. Three dining rooms at the inn serve all meals and overlooks the lake and beautiful gardens.

> 1200 Paint Rock Rd., Kingston, TN 37763
> 888-247-2464
> www.whitestoneinn.com
> $$$–$$$$$

SHOW ENTHUSIASM AND FLEXIBILITY

What I find works best may be a bit unorthodox.

Be frank about why you want to write and illustrate your book. Be sure to say something about the uniqueness and why it is important. Write up a one-or two-page proposal that sets the book in the context of your own personal interest and excitement for the project. It should come across that you are enchanted by the idea. This personal connection is what I see editors respond to in books. Years ago, an author/illustrator didn't have to show any sample art. Now, the editors want to see a piece of the book.

Do a set of thumbnail sketches to show the flow of the book and the relationship of the design and type, although it will change when the editor and book designer work on it later. Sometimes the art director is brought in immediately and other times the art director enters the picture well into the project. Be receptive and flexible to their changes.

The thumbnail sketches give you something to focus on and give you a clear idea of where to go and where not to go with your book.

I find that presenting four spreads done in pencil works the best. They could be done in color, with pen and ink, colored pencils, drafting film, etc., but the drawings should be fairly polished—whatever it takes to see how it works.

—*David Weitzman, author/illustrator of 20 books including* A Model T: How Henry Ford Built a Legend, A Subway For New York, Rama and Sita, *and* Jenny: The Airplane That Taught America to Fly

Knoxville

~Maple Grove Inn

Situated on sixteen landscaped acres, this bed and breakfast was built in 1799. It has six rooms and two suites, and all have modern details such as

TV/VCR, private baths, and art with antique furnishings. The suites include spa tubs, fireplaces, and decks or porches. A full breakfast and some dinners are included.

8800 Westland Dr., Knoxville, TN 37923
800-645-0713
www.maplegroveinn.com
$$–$$$$$

Gatlinburg
~Eight Gables Inn
Located at the entrance to the Great Smoky Mountain National Park, this lovely, country inn has twelve rooms and eight suites, all with elegant décor and amenities. All rooms have TV/VCR, feather beds, robes, and the suites have fireplaces and spa tubs. The common areas are rustically elegant with a grand staircase, parlors with fireplaces, and porches with rockers, overlooking immaculate landscaping. A full breakfast is included, and during the week, light suppers are included, as well.

219 N. Mountain Trail, Gatlinburg, TN 37738
800-279-5716
www.eightgables.com
$$$–$$$$

Monteagle
~The Adams Edgeworth Inn
This National Historic Registry inn built in 1896, sits in a wooded area, high in the Cumberland Mountains. There are eight rooms and three suites, in country décor, with private baths and clawfoot tubs, quilts, and antiques. The inn has an enormous wraparound veranda, which overlooks gardens, a large library, and a restaurant. Breakfast is included. The inn is located next to the Chautauqua Victorian Village and the Tennessee Williams Memorial Theatre.

Monteagle Assembly, Cottage #23, Monteagle, TN 37356
931-924-4000
www.relaxinn.com
$$–$$$$$

West Virginia

Hico

~Country Road Cabins

Located near the New River Gorge and Gauley River Canyon, these rustic, yet comfortable, cabins have from one-to three-bedrooms, with kitchens. Special off-season and weekly rates are available.

P.O. Box 44, Sunday Rd., Hico, WV 25884
888-712-2246
$$–$$$$$

Lewisburg

~General Lewis Inn

Located in southern West Virginia, this magnificent Colonial-style inn, owned by the same family since the 1920s, has a wonderful restaurant. The 23 rooms are furnished with antiques, canopy or poster beds, private baths, luxurious details, and two suites are available. There is a large, elegant veranda and the inn is situated near the historic district of town.

301 E. Washington St. Lewisburg, WV 24901
800-628-4454
www.generallewisinn.com
$–$$$

Parkersburg

~Blennerhassett Hotel

This National Historic Landmark hotel, located in the Ohio Valley, was built in 1889. It has five floors with 91 rooms and 14 suites, all with private baths, cable TV, data ports, room service, period furnishings, and there is a restaurant on the premises..

Market and 4th Streets, Parkersburg, WV 26101
800-262-2536
www.theblennerhassett.com
$$–$$$$

8

THE
NORTHEAST

Pennsylvania

New Jersey

New York

Connecticut

Massachusetts

Vermont

New Hampshire

Rhode Island

Maine

While it is the most densely populated area of the country, the North-east region is also one of the most beautiful and diverse, with miles of coast-line, beautiful beaches, mountains, rolling hills, and lakes. There are also big cities here, if that is what inspires you the most. This region offers places for everyone—on every budget.

Pennsylvania

Lititz

~Swiss Woods

Set on 30 acres in the Amish country of Lancaster county, this inn feels and looks like a Swiss cottage with lots of natural wood, magnificent gar-dens, hills, lake views from balconies or patios in each room and a full old-world breakfast is included. Rooms have attached private baths, two with spa tubs.

> 500 Blantz Rd., Lititz, PA 17543
> 800-594-8018
> www.swisswoods.com
> $$–$$$$

Strasburg

~Historic Strasburg Inn

Located deep in Lancaster county's Amish country, this elegant coun-try inn has 102 rooms and some suites on 58 acres of well-manicured grounds. The magnificent Colonial-style building was constructed in 1793 and it also has a fine restaurant. All rooms have private baths, antique furnishings and all the luxurious amenities of a fine hotel. There are oriental rugs and fire-places in the common rooms and in some guest rooms.

> One Historic Dr., Strasburg, PA 17579
> 800-872-0201
> www.historicstrasburginn.com
> $$–$$$$$

In the Pocono Mountains

Milford
~Pine Hill Farm B & B

This charming farmhouse has six delightful rooms decorated in Ralph Lauren style, with private baths, spa tubs, fireplaces, and some rooms have sitting areas. The rooms also feature views of the hills, the Delaware River Valley, and the gorgeous 277 acre grounds surrounding the inn. A full breakfast is included.

181 Pine Hill Farm Rd., Milford, PA 18337
570-296-5261
www.pinehillfarm.com
$$–$$$$

IT'S A BUSINESS

Publishing is a business, like any other, that requires discipline and professionalism in addition to talent and creativity. Get lots of regular feedback from people who will give you insightful, honest comments, such as a writing group or a professional editor. Treat your writing like a business, and imagine yourself as the CEO.

Network furiously and recruit talented people whose skills complement yours such as an agent, editor or publicist to your "team". And most important, put pen to paper or fingers to keyboard and write—every day.

—*Ted Weinstein, literary agent.*

South Sterling
~The French Manor

This elegant country estate, constructed of stone has fifteen luxurious rooms, all with private baths (eight are suites with fireplaces and spa tubs). Many rooms have balconies, and breakfast and tea are served on the lovely veranda. Complimentary sherry, fruit, and cheese are served in the evening, and the inn's restaurant serves French cuisine for dinner.

> Huckleberry Rd., South Sterling, PA 18460
> 800-523-8200
> www.thefrenchmanor.com
> $$–$$$$$

Wilkes Barre
~The Woodlands Inn & Resort
The Pocono Mountains afford many places to stay, but this resort is located on acres of wooded grounds, with several different kinds of accommodations, and all luxurious amenities.

> 1073 Hwy. 315, Wilkes Barre, PA 18702
> 800-762-2222
> www.thewoodlandsresort.com
> $$—$$$$

New Hope
~The Whitehall Inn
New Hope is a charming town on the Delaware River right across from New Jersey and close to Philadephia in Buck's county. This bed and breakfast was built in 1794 and has six wonderful rooms with private baths and fireplaces. It is well known for the wonderful cuisine, including a four-course candlelit breakfast, afternoon tea and chocolates, all served on fine china, are included in the room price. A pool, surrounded by lovely gardens, make this a perfect hideaway.

> 1370 Pineville Rd., New Hope, PA 18938
> 215-598-7945
> $$$–$$$$

Holicong
~Barley Sheaf Farm
This lovely Colonial-style inn, with eight rooms and five suites, sits on 30 acres in Buck's County, near New Hope. Formerly the home of playwright George S. Kaufman, the rooms are well-appointed, with private baths, some with spa tubs and fireplaces, and all rooms include a full breakfast and afternoon refreshments.

5281 York Rd., Holicong, PA 18928
215-794-5104
www.barleysheaf.com
$$–$$$$$

New Jersey

Egg Harbor City
~Tuscany House at Renault Winery

Yes, there really is a Mediterranean-style winery and hotel in South Jersey. The Renault winery is actually one of the oldest continuously operating wineries in the country and the owners recently built this beautiful 50-room inn and restaurant. The rooms are luxurious, with private baths and all the amenities of a fine hotel, which resembles an Italian villa.

2111 Bremen Ave., Egg Harbor City, NJ 08215
609-965-7948
www.renaultwinery.com
$$–$$$$

Cape May
~Humphrey Hughes House

A quaint beach town near the Delaware border, filled with historic Victorian buildings, Cape May is best visited in off-season, meaning not in the summer. This lovely bed and breakfast in the middle of the historic district has bigger rooms than most of the inns in town, with private baths, antique furnishings, TV, and air conditioning. The veranda overlooks the ocean and well-manicured gardens, and a full breakfast and afternoon tea are served.

29 Ocean St., Cape May, NJ 08204
800-582-3634
www.humphreyhugheshouse.com
$$–$$$$$

~The Queen Victoria

There are two buildings at this bed and breakfast inn right in the center of the town's historic district. In total, there are fifteen rooms and six suites, all with private baths, air conditioning, refrigerators, and quilts. Some rooms have lovely antique furnishings and spa tubs and fireplaces. A large breakfast, an afternoon reception, and refreshments throughout the evening are complimentary.

> 102 Ocean St., Cape May, NJ 08204
> 609-884-8702
> www.queenvictoria.com
> $$–$$$$$

ASSUME NOTHING

The best proposals are those that elicit the fewest questions. Why? Because you've anticipated and answered them all.

—*Jane von Mehren, executive editor, Penguingroup, from* Editors on Editing.

Princeton
~Nassau Inn
Located in the charming, historic downtown, near Princeton University, the Colonial-style Nassau Inn, built in 1756, has 203 elegantly-appointed rooms, decorated in warm earth tone colors and contemporary furnishings. All rooms have private baths, air conditioning, robes, safes, phones, room-service, and there is a full business center, fitness room and freshly made chocolate chip cookies are available daily. Shops and restaurants are just steps away.

> 10 Palmer Square, Princeton, NJ 08542
> 800-862-7728
> $$$$–$$$$$

Spring Lake
~The Breakers
Only a little over an hour's drive from New York City, you will find this lively beach town on the Jersey shore. The only oceanfront hotel in the area, The Breakers is a small, historic hotel, with wraparound verandas and spectacular ocean views. It also has a pool and restaurant. All rooms

have private baths, TV, phones, refrigerators, air conditioning, and comfortable furnishings. Suites have spa tubs, and most rooms have fabulous beach and ocean views.

1507 Ocean Ave., Spring Lake, NJ 07762
732-449-7700
www.breakershotel.com
$–$$$$$

~Sea Crest By The Sea

There are eight beautiful rooms at this bed and breakfast by the ocean, with private baths, TV/VCR, featherbeds, air conditioning, refrigerators, and elegant amenities, including a candlelit breakfast.

19 Tuttle Ave., Spring Lake, NJ 07762
800-803-9031
www.seacrestbythesea.com
$$$$$

New York

New York City

According to a line in the Broadway show *Gypsy*, "New York is the center of everything." It certainly has many diverse areas, from mountains to ocean, as well as being the largest, most cosmopolitan city in America, and I have included lodgings both in and out of the city.

Manhattan

There are five boroughs in the city of New York. Manhattan island is the area with Wall Street, Broadway, Times Square, and most of the major tourist attractions. For people who want city sounds, or live in Manhattan and need to escape their homes without leaving the island, here are some suggestions:

~Algonquin Hotel

This is an historic, charming 174-room hotel, with a powerful literary past, located in the heart of midtown.

59 W. 44th St., New York, NY 10036
212-840-6800, 888-304-2047
$$$–$$$$

~Gramercy Park Hotel

This hotel was built in the 1920s; Humphrey Bogart was married here and John F. Kennedy stayed here as a young man. Many of the 509 rooms and suites face the charming Gramercy Park, the only private square in the city. Hotel guests receive a key to enjoy the park, and continental breakfast is included. There are spacious rooms, private baths, air conditioning, and business services are available, including high-speed Internet access. A bar and restaurant are located on the premises.

2 Lexington Ave., New York, NY 10010
800-221-4083
www.gramercyparkhotel.com
$$$–$$$$$

~Hotel Wolcott

This basic 65-room hotel is located in midtown. Every room has a desk, but accommodations are simple.

4 W. 31 St. New York, NY 10001
212-268-2900
www.wolcott.com
$$–$$$

~The Lombardy

Located in midtown, this small hotel was built in 1926. The 40 rooms and 75 suites are individually decorated with no two alike. The rooms have modern amenities, such as data ports with dual phone lines, marble bathrooms, and walk-in closets. There is a fitness room, concierge service, and an elegant lobby and bar.

111 E. 56th St., New York, NY 10022
212-753-8600
$$$$$

GREAT WRITERS ARE GREAT READERS

The most common problem I encounter with new, aspiring writers, particularly novelists, is their general lack of familiarity with the books and writers that have gone before them. One would expect, as certainly publishers expect, that a mystery writer would be familiar with not only the general forms and tropes of the mystery genre, but would also have read widely in the genre. For a new mystery writer working today to not have read Dennis Lehane, Michael Connelly, P.D. James, Patricia Cornwall, Ian Rankin, Walter Mosely, and a dozen or so others, simply means that he is not serious about his craft or genre. By the same token, a literary novelist unfamiliar with the great writing of the past, not to say the best of the current generation, is probably a poseur, is certainly disrespectful of the craft, and is unlikely to have much of interest to say.

By and large, great writers are great readers. Too many of the aspiring writers I meet seem to take pride in their ignorance, or, almost worse, have fastened onto one model to imitate.

So, the advice I find I give most frequently is two-fold: Read, read like mad, widely, passionately, and critically. Take risks in your reading and make it a part of your writing life. And, two, haunt the places where books are read, bought, and sold. Learn what others are reading and why. Don't be afraid to actually buy a book now and then, as well. It all adds to the mix.

—*John Silbersack, senior vice president and literary agent (Trident Media Group)*

~Milburn Hotel

This small hotel is located on a quiet street on the Upper West Side near the famous deli, Zabar's. Unlike most of the city's hotels, the rooms are spacious and, in fact, they are all suites that feel more like apartments, with fully equipped kitchens. Some are studios and others are one-bedroom. There are TVs, phones, air conditioning, private baths, tables, desks, and comfortable furnishings.

242 W. 76th St., New York, NY 10023
212-362-1006
$$$–$$$$

~The Regency Hotel

Located on the Upper East Side, this luxurious hotel recently underwent a $35 million dollar renovation, and the 350 rooms and suites are beautifully appointed with mahogany furnishings, featherbeds, safes, fax machines, and all have private, marble bathrooms. The service is impeccable here, with 24-hour room service, 24-hour limousine service, a full business center and a large fitness center, which includes a spa and sauna. The lounge, serving beverages and light snacks, is called "The Library."

> 540 Park Ave., New York, NY 10021
> 212-759-4100
> **$$$$$**

~ThirtyThirty Hotel

Located right in the middle of the East Side, near the Empire State Building, this renovated hotel with 300 rooms is modern, yet comfortable. All rooms have private baths, and some rooms have work areas, sitting areas, data ports, radio with CD player, and in-room dining. High-speed Internet access is available.

> 30 E. 30th St., New York, NY 10016
> 800-497-6028
> 212-689-1900
> www.stayinNY.com
> **$$$–$$$$$**

Long Island

This part of New York is filled with beautiful beaches on both the north and south shores, but avoid summers here as they are filled with New York City folk escaping the heat. Best known of the beach areas is the Hamptons. Long known for its trendy appeal, ritzy clubs and restaurants, and expensive celebrity homes, this is a wonderful spot for creative people to visit. The natural beauty, small, historic towns, and magnificent beaches offer writers and artists numerous places to seduce the muse.

Port Jefferson
~HollyBerry Bed & Breakfast

Located on the harborfront of the North Shore, yet only one hour from

New York City, this restored 1800s farm house has air-conditioned suites, with flowers and antique furnishings and private baths. A candlelit breakfast is included, and it is a short walk to the shops and restaurants in this quaint town.

415 W. Broadway, Port Jefferson, NY 11777
631-331-3123
$$–$$$

Woodbury
~The Inn at Fox Hollow
This is a luxurious all-suite hotel in the middle of Long Island. The 145 suites have full kitchens, private baths with marble and granite and soaking tubs, high-speed Internet access, and the inn has a pool, spa and fitness center, and complimentary breakfast and a weekday light supper are included.

7755 Jericho Turnpike, Woodbury, NY 11797
800-291-8090
www.theinnatfoxhollow.com
$$$–$$$$$

The Hamptons

Amagansett
~Gansett Greeen Manor
Located on two lovely acres with gardens, ponds and patios, this inn has eight suites and four cottages. All have private baths, private entrances, TV, kitchens with barbecues, and pets are allowed. It is a mere few blocks to the beach.

273 Main St., Amagansett, NY 11930
631-267-3133
www.gansettgreenmanor.com
$$$$$

East Hampton
~Mill House Inn
This is a luxurious eight-room bed and breakfast built in 1790, located

near the shops and restaurants of this charming village, and about a mile from the ocean. All the rooms are outfitted with the finest furnishings, such as featherbeds, fine linens, antique furnishings, art, leather couches, flat screen TV/DVD/CD, stereo, wet bar, fireplace, air conditioning, phones, upscale toiletries, and more. Deluxe rooms contain spa tubs, and gourmet breakfast and afternoon refreshments are included and served overlooking the magnificent gardens. Good dogs are allowed.

> 31 N. Main St., East Hampton, NY 11937
> 631-324-9766
> www.millhouseinn.com
> **$$$–$$$$$**

Southampton
~Southampton Inn
Located right in town on five gorgeous acres of flowers and lawns, this hotel has ninety rooms, all elegantly-appointed, with luxurious amenities. All rooms have refrigerators, data ports, phones, and desks. There is a library and parlor room with a fireplace, an outdoor heated pool, a fitness center, and bed and breakfast packages are available.

> 91 Hill St., Southampton, NY 11968
> 800-832-6500
> www.southamptoninn.com
> **$$–$$$$$**

~Village Latch Inn Hotel
Located on a beautiful estate setting, and serving visitors since 1901, this property actually has four separate buildings, but the main house has 24 rooms. Filled with antiques, art, and fireplaces, the rooms all have private baths and luxurious amenities.

> 101 Hill St., Southampton, NY 11968
> 800-54-LATCH
> www.villagelatch.com
> **$$$$–$$$$$**

Montauk

~Gurney's Inn Resort & Spa

This is one of the original beachfront inns in the Hamptons, with 109 rooms, most with great ocean views, an indoor pool, fitness center, restaurant/lounge, and comfortable rooms with private baths and all the basic necessities.

> 290 Old Montauk Hwy., Montauk, NY.11954
> 631-668-2345
> $$$$$

Shelter Island

~Dering Harbor Inn

Only a two-hour trip from New York City, this 20 room inn has some kitchenettes, and all rooms have private baths, TV, voice mail, hair dryers, air conditioning, decks overlooking the harbor, and the inn is close to the ferry. There is a salt-water pool and tennis court.

> 13 Winthrop Rd., Shelter Island, NY 11965
> 631-749-0900
> www.deringharborinn.com
> $$$–$$$$$

ISLAND HIDEAWAY

My favorite place to hide away is Shelter Island, New York. There is no movie theater, just a couple of decent restaurants and woods. The surf doesn't pound here—ever. Simply listen to the gentle waves and sit under the shade. There are some charming bed and breakfasts and inns right in town. It is best to come to the island in the winter—and only by ferry. It is off the north fork of Long Island, and once you are off the ferry, I suggest you rent one of the electric carts to get around.

—*Clare Ferraro, president of Viking/Plume, a division of the PenguinGroup and publisher of Dorothy Allison, Garrison Keillor and Dave Pelzer*

Eastport

~Seatuck Cove House

Located near the Hamptons, this five-room bed and breakfast is situated on the water, with a private beach at a marina. All the rooms have private baths, satellite TV, sitting rooms, and balconies overlooking the water. There is a heated pool, lovely common rooms, and breakfast is included at this lovely New England-style inn.

> 61 S. Bay Ave., Eastport, NY 11941
> 631-325-3300
> www.seatuckcovehouse.com
> $$$–$$$$$

Upstate New York

Within two hours of New York City, the following inns are all viable by train.

Cold Spring

~Pig Hill Inn

This is a beautiful, brick mansion in a charming town on the Hudson River, only about an hour north of Manhattan and a few blocks walk from the train station so no car is necessary. Five rooms have private baths and lovely furnishings, from Chippendate to Chinoisevir antiques, which are for sale. A full breakfast is included and can be brought to your bed or taken in the Victorian conservatory.

> 73 Main St., Cold Spring, NY 10516
> 845-265-9247
> www.pighillinn.com
> $$–$$$$

Garrison

~The Bird & Bottle Inn

A historic Hudson Valley Colonial-style country inn, built in 1761, it is best known for its fine restaurant, which is open Wed-Sun. There are three rooms and one cottage, all beautifully decorated with antique furnishings, canopy beds, fireplaces, and all have private baths. Continental breakfast is included on weekdays.

1183 Old Albany Post Rd., Garrison, NY 10524
800-782-6837
www.birdbottle.com
$$$$–$$$$$

Rhinebeck
~The Beekman Arms

This historic inn and village are charming. Listed on the National Registry of Historic Buildings, the inn has 63 rooms, located in the main house and the carriage houses. It is thought that George Washington slept here. Rooms are individually decorated with antiques and some fireplaces, and then have private baths, TV, phones and air conditioning. The inn has a fine restaurant on the premises and a lovely courtyard between the buildings.

Rte. 9, Rhinebeck, NY 12572
800-361-6517
www.beekmanarms.com
$–$$$

Adirondacks
(North of Albany)

Lake George
~Chelka Lodge

There are numerous places to stay along magnificent 32-mile Lake George, but this is my favorite, as I spent some childhood vacations here with my family. Renovated wood buildings make this even lovelier today, with its 25 units all facing the lake on the private beach, with trees surrounding it. All rooms have private baths, most have kitchenettes or refrigerators, air conditioning, cable TV, and a fishing dock, and boats are available. A light breakfast is served in the summer.

4204 Lake Shore Dr., Diamond Point, NY 12824
518-668-4677
www.chelkalodge.com
$–$$$

~The Sagamore

This large-scale landmark hotel is located on a private island on Lake George. There are 350 luxurious rooms and suites and all the diversions of a big resort, and there are some fabulous views of the lake from many rooms and fine restaurants. Business services are available.

> 110 Sagamore Rd., Bolton Landing, NY 12814
> 800-358-3585
> www.thesagamore.com
> $$–$$$$$

Lake Placid

~Interlaken Inn

This is a charming lake town and was home to the 1932 and 1980 winter Olympics. The blue and white country inn has eleven rooms with private baths and cozy rooms near the lake. The restaurant in the building is wonderful and there is bed and breakfast service on Tuesdays and Wednesdays when the restaurant is closed.

> 15 Interlaken Ave, Lake Placid, NY 12946
> 800-428-4369
> $–$$$$$

~Mirror Lake Inn Resort & Spa

This gorgeous Colonial-style white inn is located on a bluff overlooking Mirror Lake, which is the lake right in town. Shops and restaurants are steps away and most of the rooms have balconies with lake and town views. There are 128 elegant rooms, all with private bath and luxurious furnishings and the basic amenities, as well as cable TV, hair dryers and irons. There are heated pools, sauna, spa and other activities, such as boating, as well as spa services, business services and the restaurant on the premises is highly rated.

> 5 Mirror Lake Dr., Lake Placid, NY 12946
> 518-523-2544
> www.mirrorlakeinn.com
> $$$–$$$$$

Mirror Lake Inn Resort & Spa, Lake Placid, NY. Set on a hill, this is a charming inn with a gourmet restaurant overlooking Mirror Lake, and the inn is only one block from shops and restaurants. Courtesy of Andrea Brown

~Hilton Lake Placid Resort

The main reason to stay at this chain hotel is for the views from the rooms in the "lakefront" building. The rooms literally sit above Mirror Lake and the lake views are magnificent. Otherwise, it is your typical large hotel with five floors and 180 rooms, with private baths and the usual details. There are two heated pools, a fitness room, sauna, spa, business services, and a restaurant/lounge.

> One Mirror Lake Dr., Lake Placid, NY 12946
> 518-523-4411, 800-755-5598
> www.Hilton.com
> $–$$$$$

Saranac Lake
~The Hotel Saranac

Located in the center of this historic village, one block from the lake, this 92-room historic hotel has been welcoming visitors since 1927 and is used as a training facility for the local Paul Smith's College. Rooms have private baths and all the expected details. Business services are available and there is a restaurant on the premises.

> 101 Main St., Saranac Lake, NY 12983
> 800-937-0211
> www.hotelsaranac.com
> $–$$$

Hilton Lake Placid Resort, Lake Placid, NY. Rooms in the building atop Mirror Lake provide the soothing feeling of floating on water at this otherwise typical large hotel chain. Courtesy of Andrea Brown

Schroon Lake
~Silver Spruce Inn
This elegant lodge and bed and breakfast was originally built in the 1790s and was totally renovated in the 1930s. Only 86 miles north of Albany on the Northway, this 23-room inn, on 16 landscaped garden acres, has private baths, antique furnishings with lots of cedar paneling, and a grand common room with a sunporch and gazebo. A full breakfast is included.

> Rte. 9, P.O. Box 426, Schroon Lake, NY 12870
> 518-532-7031

www.silverspruce.com
$–$$$

Saratoga Springs
~Adelphi Hotel

This beautiful, four-story Victorian inn was built in 1877 and has been impeccably kept. With 39 units, some two-bedroom suites, and all with private baths, cable TV, and antique furnishings, this is a delightful inn with a small, heated pool.

365 Broadway, Saratoga Springs, NY 12866
518-587-4688
$$–$$$$$

LAKES AND LITERATI

Saratoga Springs, New York is a place for literati to love. Enjoy the opulence of a bygone era. Transport yourself back to the Gilded Age as you take a turn past the many beautiful mansions and inns of its main thoroughfare. As you puzzle over a plot point and logic out your storyline, luxuriate in the waters of its healing mineral springs.

Stroll the grounds at Yaddo—famed for its mission to support creative artists and its public rose gardens—a place to contemplate and cogitate (and smell the roses). Stay at the Adelphi, Batcheller Mansion Inn, Saratoga Arms or Fox n' Hound, which combine turn-of-the-century elegance with modern day amenities. Immerse yourself in health, history and horses (the town motto). While away the day finding ways to propel your tale and compel your readers.

Nestled at the foothills of the gorgeous Adirondacks, with its own special ambience of high Victoriana, is lovely Spa City, sure to inspire you and your wordsmithery.

—Katharine Sands, author and literary agent (Sarah Jane Freyman Literary Agency)

~Westchester House

This lovely, seven room Queen Anne Victorian bed and breakfast, built in 1885, is located in a quiet neighborhood surrounded by lush gardens. The opulent common rooms have high ceilings, lots of wood furnishings and

rooms have private baths, lace curtains, antique furnishings, and such modern amenities as CD players. A full continental breakfast is included. The inn is closed all of December and January.

> 102 Lincoln Ave., Saratoga Springs, NY 12866
> 800-581-7613
> www.westchesterhousebandb.com
> $$–$$$$$

Westchester House, Saratoga, NY. Located in one of the most charming towns in upstate New York, a visit to this inn is best after the summer crowds leave, and when the trees begin to turn autumnal colors.

Finger Lakes Region

Cooperstown

~Inn at Cooperstown

Built in the 1870s and renovated in the 1980s, this charming inn has seventeen rooms, all with private baths and quaint, comfortable furnishings. A continental breakfast and afternoon refreshments are included. Sitting on the large veranda in a rocking chair overlooking Otsego Lake is inspirational.

16 Chestnut St., Cooperstown, NY 13326
800-437-6303
www.innatcooperstown.com
$$–$$$$$

Inn at Cooperstown, Cooperstown, NY. Best known as the city with the Baseball Hall of Fame, this is a wonderful lakeside spot, especially during the fall foliage season. Courtesy of David Spiselman

Skaneateles

~Hobbit Hollow Farm

This magnificently restored Colonial farmhouse, situated on over 300 acres, is right on Skaneateles Lake, not far from Syracuse or Ithaca. The grounds have trails and horses to ride. There are five rooms, four with private baths. All are beautifully decorated with antique furnishings and elegant amenities. A hearty, full breakfast is included.

3061 W. Lake Rd., Skaneateles, NY 13156
800-374-3796
www.hobbithollow.com
$$–$$$$$

Connecticut

Hartford
~The Goodwin Hotel
This landmark hotel, located in the historic district of Hartford, has 124 rooms and suites. J.P. Morgan owned the building and in 1989, the hotel was totally renovated, so it is now a luxurious mix of European and Modern styles, including private baths of marble. Rooms have built-in armoires, antique furnishings, and modern business amenities are available. There is a fitness room and restaurant.

One Haynes St., Hartford, CT 06103
www.goodwinhotel.com
860-246-7500
$$$$–$$$$$

Mystic
~House of 1833 Bed & Breakfast
This seaside town, halfway between New York City and Boston, has several nice places to stay, but this inn, built in 1833 and renovated in 1994, is beautiful and soothing. The Greek Revival mansion has lush gardens and a pool, and all rooms have fireplaces, air conditioning, and private baths in all the rooms and some have spa tubs and canopy beds. Breakfast is included.

72 N. Stonington Rd., Mystic, CT 06355
800-FOR-1833
$$–$$$$$

Norfolk
~Manor House
Near the Massachusetts border, by the Berkshires, sits this historic Tudor-style mansion dating from 1898, with nine rooms, all with private baths.

Rooms are comfortable and elegant, some have fireplaces and spa tubs, and two have balconies overlooking the magnificent grounds and gardens. There is a library and dining room, where breakfast and refreshments are complimentary.

> 69 Maple Ave., Norfolk, CT 06058
> 860-542-5690
> www.manorhouse-norfolk.com
> $$–$$$$

BE REJECTION PROOF

It's best to pitch your novel when you already have a finished manuscript and not before, as an interested editor may be gone from the publishing house by the time your manuscript is finished.

Make the manuscript rejection-proof before sending it out. Pick up the pacing and strengthen your characterization. When your characters have come alive and your plot has thickened, go over your manuscript one last time to look for typos, grammatical mistakes, etc.

It's important to target your submission to the right publisher, so study the bookstore shelves. See who publishes what it is you are writing. If you see Warner Books publishes suspense and suspense is what you write, you might have a fit. If you don't have an agent, send a query letter with a two-page synopsis and a self-addressed, stamped envelope. If you have no agent and send more than a query letter, the material will come right back to you.

—*Beth de Guzman, editorial director of Mass Market Books, Warner Books*

Ridgefield
~West Lane Inn
Located on the New York state border, this elegant country inn has won many prestigious awards. Its fourteen rooms all have private baths, four-poster beds, cable TV, modem and phone hook-ups, and beautiful, luxurious individual furnishings. Some rooms have fireplaces and kitchenettes. A continental breakfast is included.

22 W. Lane, Ridgefield, CT 06877
203-438-7323
www.westlaneinn.com
$$$–$$$$$

Massachusetts

The Berkshires

Located on the borders of New York, Vermont, and Connecticut, this area has mountains, art, culture, fine colleges, great restaurants, lakes, and wonderful inns.

Lenox
~*The Village Inn*

Lenox is a quaint and charming village in the true New England tradition and there are several wonderful inns here. This one dates from 1771 and still retains the charm of that era, with antique furnishings in the common rooms as well as in the 32 guest rooms, all with private baths, canopy beds, phone, TV/VCR/radio, spa tubs, and there are fireplaces in some rooms. A full breakfast and afternoon tea are included in the room price.

16 Church St., Lenox, MA 01240
800-253-0917
www.villageinn-lenox.com
$–$$$$$

North Adams
~*Porches Inn*

This most unusual inn actually is six newly remodeled Victorian style row houses that are fully wired for modern travelers. The 52 large rooms have DSL hook-ups, and vintage lamps and private baths. There is a heated pool, sauna, spa and fitness room. Continental breakfast is included and the new Massachusetts Museum of Contemporary Art is right across the street.

231 River St., North Adams, MA 01247
413-664-0400

www.porches.com
$$$–$$$$

Stockbridge

~The Inn at Stockbridge

This elegant turn-of-the-century Colonial mansion, has eight rooms and eight suites, all with private baths, and is located on over 10 acres of beautiful grounds. Some suites have fireplaces and spa tubs and the common rooms downstairs are gracious and warm. A full breakfast, wine and snacks are complimentary.

Rte. 7N, Stockbridge, MA 01262
888-466-7865
www.stockbridgeinn.com
$$–$$$$$

Cape Cod and the Coast

Chatham

~Captain's House Inn

Cape Cod, just a short ride from the Boston area, is a peninsula that sticks out into the Atlantic Ocean and is filled with charming beach towns to visit. Do avoid the summer here. The village of Chatham, at the lower end of the peninsula, is one of the quieter, quainter towns. This beautiful and historic bed and breakfast was built in 1839 on over two acres of well manicured grounds. The twelve rooms and four suites all have private baths, four-poster beds, TV/VCR, phones, air conditioning, and the suites have fireplaces, coffee, refrigerators, and spa tubs. A hearty breakfast, afternoon tea, and refreshments are included.

369 Old Harbor Rd., Chatham, MA 02633
800-315-0728
www.captainshouseinn.com
$$$–$$$$$

Eastham

~Whalewalk Inn

Located on a quiet, secluded road near Orleans Village, this former captain's home from the 1830s is now a beautiful bed and breakfast with eleven rooms and five suites, all with private baths. The rooms are in different buildings scattered throughout the three acres of beautifully landscaped grounds. Rooms are individually decorated with antique and period furnishings and have air conditioning, TV/VCR, phones, and the suites have spa tubs. A full breakfast and late day refreshments are included.

220 Bridge Rd., Eastham, MA 02642
800-440-1281
www.whalewalkinn.com
$$$-$$$$$

Vermont

This is one of the most beautiful states for reflecting, writing and creating, with its mountains, open spaces, and glorious fall foliage. Fall and winter are the busy seasons here, so it is crowded and expensive from September till the end of February.

Burlington
~Willard Street Inn

One of the largest of Vermont's cities, Burlington is located at the northern end on Lake Champlain. This inn dating from the 1880s is situated close to downtown and has views of the lake and the Adirondacks. It is one of the most historic buildings in this part of the state, with its unique Georgian/Victorian/Revival style architecture and cherrywood-paneled hallway. All 14 rooms have private baths, featherbeds, individualized antique furnishings, cable TV, and air conditioning. Most of the rooms have fabulous lake views. Breakfast, with entrees such as eggs benedict, is complimentary and served overlooking lovely gardens in the solarium.

349 S. Willard St., Burlington, VT 05401
800-577-8712
www.willardstreetinn.com
$$-$$$$

Chittenden

~Fox Creek Inn

This is a picturesque country inn, surrounded by woods and mountains, near Rutland, has nine elegant rooms, all with private baths and many with spa tubs and fireplaces. There is a storybook charm here and a full breakfast is served, as well as candlelit dinners for an extra charge.

> 49 Dam Rd., Chittenden, VT 05737
> 800-707-0017
> www.foxcreekinn.com
> $$$–$$$$$

Putney

~The Putney Inn

This estate in southern Vermont has been around since the 1750s and now boasts 25 charming rooms, with private baths, some with private entrances (in the carriage house building), phones, cable TV, air conditioning, poster beds, lots of beamed ceilings, and antique furnishings throughout. A hearty breakfast is included, and the inn's restaurant is highly-rated.

> P. O. Box 181, Putney, VT 05346
> 800-653-5517
> www.putneyinn.com
> $$–$$$

WHAT'S A FEW MOSQUITOS?

Vermont is beautiful, except for the mosquitos in the summer—bring plenty of bug spray. It is the perfect spot for writers and artists to get and stay inspired.

—Sandra Beriss, copy editor and author of several children's books

Stowe

~Auberge de Stowe

A charming, rambling house with five comfortable rooms with private baths. There is a pool and large breakfast room and sitting room with TV, and the owner, Chantal, bakes fresh food daily for the full, included breakfast. The inn is a short walk to the shops and restaurants in town. Pets and children are allowed.

>692 S. Main St., Stowe, VT 05672
>800-387-8789
>www.aubergedestowe.com
>$$–$$$

RETREAT TO A CONFERENCE

Attend writers conferences, and, besides meeting agents, try to find an opportunity to see at least one editor who handles your genre. Get lots of feedback on your work. You should learn something useful from each conference. Go home and think about the feedback you got. Look at your material with fresh eyes. Make your work better. Rewrite and polish your presentation before sending your material out. This improves your chances for getting your work published.

—*Susan Crawford, literary agent (Crawford Literary Agency)*

~Trapp Family Lodge

Yes, if you are a fan of *The Sound of Music*, this is the lodge for you. Its motto is "A little of Austria. A lot of Vermont." The original Trapp family bought this large resort with gorgeous mountain views, several restaurants and plenty of recreational facilities. The rooms are well-appointed, with private baths, air conditioning, phones, and all the basics. It may be too disruptive with many families around, but it is unique.

>700 Trapp Hill Rd., Stowe, VT 05672
>800-826-7000
>www.trappfamily.com
>$$$$–$$$$$

Woodstock
~The Woodstock Inn

Located in one of the most charming villages in the whole country, both this inn and the town are historic. The 142 rooms are spacious, elegantly-appointed, with modern amenities, built-in bookshelves and 23 rooms have fireplaces. The grounds and gardens are stunning, as are the views. There are four restaurants at the inn and a fitness center, and business services are available.

> Fourteen The Green, Woodstock, VT 05091
> 800-448-7900
> www.woodstockinn.com
> $$$–$$$$$

New Hampshire

The White Mountains of New Hampshire have numerous places to stay and many quaint towns.

Holderness
~Manor on Golden Pond
Located in the center of the state, with views of Squam Lake, this English style manor house has 25 rooms with private baths, and individualized décor. Many rooms have fireplaces or spa tubs and decks overlooking the lake. The common rooms include a library and a dining room with magnificent natural wood. Breakfast is included and the restaurant is excellent for dinner.

> Rt. 3, Holderness, NH 03245
> 800-545-2141
> www.manorongoldenpond.com
> $$$$–$$$$$

Jackson
~Dana Place Inn
This country inn was built in the 1890s, and all the 35 charming rooms have private baths and luxurious amenities, and there is a pool and spa. Some rooms have views of the Ellis River. The inn is famous for its great food and breakfast is included in the room price.

Rt. 16, Jackson, NH 03846
800-537-9276
www.danaplace.com
$$$–$$$$$

~Christmas Farm Inn

This Colonial-style inn, on over ten acres, has 41 rooms and some cottages are available with spa tubs and fireplaces. All the rooms have private baths and cozy, comfortable furnishings and some have balconies. The restaurant is excellent and serves all meals. Bed and breakfast and meal plans are available. Sleigh rides are also available.

Route 16B, Jackson, NH 03846
800-HI-ELVES
www.christmasfarminn.com
$$$–$$$$$

North Conway
~The Farm by the River B & B

This beautiful farmhouse inn, built in 1771, lies by the Saco River on 70 acres of hills and pastures. The ten rooms, all have private baths, are decorated with family heirlooms, lace curtains over windows with views of the White Mountains and the river, air conditioning, and some rooms have spa tubs and fireplaces. A full breakfast is included.

2555 West Side Rd., North Conway, NH, 03860
888-414-8353
www.farmbytheriver.com
$$–$$$$

Rhode Island

Block Island
~The 1661 Inn

There is nothing quite like having your own island, but this is pretty close and an easy ferry ride from either Rhode Island or New York, as it is in the middle of both. This New England-style inn has many rooms with ocean views or decks, some have spa tubs and/or fireplaces, but all have private baths and TVs. The Hotel Manisses is located next door, with a fabulous restaurant. Breakfast is included.

P.O. Box 1, Block Island, RI 02807

800-626-4773

$–$$$$$

Farm By the River B & B, NH. Artist-owned, this bed and breakfast also provides stables with horseback riding. Courtesy of Farm By the River B & B

Newport
~Castle Hill Inn & Resort

Historic and charming Newport was the playground of the rich and famous and this hotel exemplifies that tradition today. Located high on a cliff, on forty acres, the inn has 25 totally elegant rooms, all with magnificent views of the ocean and bay. All have private marble baths with large spa tubs, king beds with fine linens, fireplaces, antiques and oriental rugs, sitting areas, and top-of-the-line service. Complimentary breakfast and afternoon tea are served on fine china, overlooking the water.

> 590 Ocean Dr., Newport, RI 02840
> 888-466-1355
> www.castlehillinn.com
> $$$$$

Providence
~Old Court Inn
Located next to the capitol building, this ten-room inn used to be a rectory when built in 1863. Now its ten rooms are all beautifully renovated, with hardwood floors, private baths, high ceilings, brass beds, marble fireplaces, phones, and TV, as well as city views. Breakfast is included.

> 144 Benefit St., Providence, RI 02903
> 401-751-2002
> www.oldcourt.com
> $$–$$$

Maine

Stretching from the northern coast to the southern coast and bordering a tiny piece of New Hampshire coastline, Maine is a creative person's paradise.

Bar Harbor
~Manor House Inn
Located at the northern part of Maine, close to the Canadian border, this unique coastal town also has the beautiful Acadia National Park. It is the perfect getaway place, as it is quiet, and low-key, yet soothing and scenic. This fourteen-room Victorian inn is on the National Register of Historic Places. All rooms have private baths and period furnishings, dating from the

1880s, yet all the basic modern amenities. A full breakfast and afternoon refreshments are included.

106 West St., Bar Harbor, ME 04609
800-437-0088
www.barharbormanorhouse.com
$–$$$$

LIBRARY AS MINI-RETREAT

Even if you can't ditch the family or afford travel, there is usually a public library within a close drive of most people's homes. Mornings are usually dead zones, with maybe only a few seniors around, so find a quiet study area in the library, claim a desk, spread out, and you can work for hours anonymously. After three o'clock, it becomes the school zone.

—*Jeff Herman, literary agent and author of* The Writer's Guide To Book Editors, Publishers and Literary Agents. *He lives in Massachusetts*

Blue Hill

~Blue Hill Inn

Located by Deer Isle and overlooking Blue Hill Bay, this clapboard inn was built in 1840, and it has eleven rooms and one suite. All rooms have private baths and some contain clawfoot tubs. There are antique furnishings, down comforters, and a full breakfast, as well as afternoon refreshments, are included.

40 Union St., Blue Hill, ME 04614
800-826-7415
www.bluehillinn.com
$$$–$$$$$

Boothbay

~Hodgdon Island Inn

The harbor at Boothbay is filled with lobster boats, as well as wonderful artists' studios, where handcrafted products are created. This New England-style inn, just five minutes from town, dates from 1810, when it was a sea captain's home. Now restored, the eight rooms all have private baths, four-poster beds, and cove water views.

A full breakfast is included, amid original art from New England artists such as Ed Betts, Michael Palmer, and DeWitt Hardy, and the porch has white wicker furniture overlooking the cove.

> Barters Island Rd., P.O. Box 492, Boothbay, ME 04571
> 207-633-7474
> www.hodgdonislandinn.com
> $$–$$$

Kennebunkport
~Captain Lord Mansion
Summer home of the George Bush family, this is the kind of town you expect in Maine, quaint, charming and along the water. This sixteen-room bed and breakfast, located on a hill overlooking the Kennebunk River, is elegant, with magnificent antique furnishings, fresh flowers, and rooms with private baths with heated marble floors, and four-poster beds. Some rooms have fireplaces and sitting areas.

> Green St. P.O. Box 800, Kennebunkport, ME 04046
> 207-967-3141
> www.captainlord.com
> $$$–$$$$$

Newcatle
~Newcastle Inn
Located on the mid-coast of Maine, this fifteen-room inn has antique furnishings, lovely gardens, and views of water. The well-appointed rooms all have private baths and some have spa tubs. Many rooms have fireplaces, canopy or four-poster beds, and sitting areas. A full breakfast and an afternoon reception are included.

> 60 River Rd., Newcastle, ME 04553
> 800-832-8669
> www.newcastleinn.com
> $$–$$$$$

Ogunquit
~Hartwell House

Located in southern Maine, this inn has sixteen rooms, suites, and studios with kitchenettes. All the rooms are spacious, with private baths and antique furnishings, and a full breakfast and afternoon tea are included and served on the sunporch overlooking gardens and Perkins Cove.

312 Shore Rd., Ogunquit, ME 03907
800-235-8883
www.hartwellhouseinn.com
$$–$$$$

THE
MID-ATLANTIC

Delaware

Maryland

Virginia

North Carolina

The mid-Atlantic and Chesapeake Bay region is known for its fabulous fresh seafood, especially the crabs. There are many wonderful areas to hideaway in along the coast and in towns along the Appalachian and Blue Ridge Mountains.

Delaware

Montchanin
~Inn at Montchanin Village

This historic inn has 27 rooms and suites in eleven restored buildings, surrounded by magnificent manicured gardens and courtyards. The rooms are furnished with antiques and artistic reproductions, and have private marble baths, robes, elegant amenities, turn-down service, and charming décor. The buildings date from 1799 through the early 1900's. There is a restaurant on the premises that used to be a blacksmith's shop. The inn is located only five miles northwest of Wilmington.

> Route 100 and Kirk Rd., Montchanin, DE 19710
> 800-269-2473
> www.montchanin.com
> $$–$$$$$

Rehoboth Beach
~Sea Witch Manor Inn & Spa

Located by the ocean in the historic part of town, but on a quiet, residential street, this five-room bed and breakfast is for adults only and has a 24-hour cordials bar, as well as a tea bar with refreshments. This charming Victorian inn also has an outdoor spa, but some of the private baths also have spa tubs. All rooms have refrigerators, and comfortable, antique furnishings.

> 71 Lake Ave., Rehoboth Beach, DE 19971
> 866-732-9482
> seawitchmanor.com
> $$$–$$$$

Maryland

Keedysville
~Antietam Overlook Farm
Overlooking four states, this western Maryland 95-acre mountain top inn has six rooms, all with private baths and some with large soaking tubs and fireplaces. Charming wood and flowered furnishings give the place a warm, homey feel and a full breakfast and beverages, available all day, are complimentary.

> P.O. Box 30, Keedysville, MD 21756
> www.antietamoverlook.com
> 800-878-4241
> $$$

Oxford
~Robert Morris Inn
This 35-room inn is located right on the Chesapeake and many of its rooms entertain great water views. The main inn was built in 1710 and there are some rooms from that time, as well as more modern rooms, but all have private baths and some have clawfoot tubs. All the basic amenities are included. There is a restaurant on the premises.

> 314 N. Morris St., Oxford, MD 21654
> 888-823-4012
> www.robertmorrisinn.com
> $$–$$$$$

Ocean City
~Quality Inn Beachfront Hotel
This may be a Quality Inn, but this 109-room hotel is new and is situated right on the beach, affording great ocean views. The suite rooms contain refrigerators, microwaves, icemakers, and spa tubs. Bedroom areas have dividers, TV, and there are large terraces. There are two pools, a spa and a fitness room on the premises.

P.O. Box 910, Ocean City, MD 21842
410-289-1234
www.qualityinnbeachfront.com
$–$$$$$

Virginia

Virginia is both historic and beautiful, with choices of ocean atmosphere or mountains and countryside. There are no listings for Washington D.C., as most creative people choose to leave the capital for Virginia locations.

Charlottesville
~Silver Thatch Inn
Built as a barracks in 1780, later a boarding school for boys, a tobacco plantation and then a farm, this elegant, clapboard inn has been welcoming guests since the 1970s. There are seven rooms, all with private baths. Rooms are elegantly-appointed and decorated with antiques. A full breakfast is included in the room price.

3001 Hollymead Dr., Charlottesville, VA 22911
800-261-0720
www.silverthatch.com
$$–$$$$

~Clifton–The Country Inn
This magnificent country manor sits on over 40 acres of gardens, manicured lawns, and a lake. There is a pool, spa, gift shop, and tennis court. The seven rooms and seven suites with antique furnishings all have private baths, fireplaces, and modern amenities, such as voicemail, CD players, and hair dryers.

1296 Clifton Inn Dr., Charlottesville, VA 22911
888-971-1800
www.cliftoninn.com
$$–$$$$$

THE KEY? WRITE ON A BREAKOUT SCALE

My favorite getaway is anywhere that is not home or office. I take my laptop to coffee bars, hotels, airports…it doesn't matter. When I switch it on, I switch on my creative side. I do not mind noise, people around, or anything else. I tune them out. Writing time is precious and I use it whenever I get it. Late at night is also good.

What should writers do to get published these days? I am an agent who specializes in fiction. Novelists need to know that the difficult thing is not *getting* published, but *staying* published. The industry today quickly washes out authors who do not find a sizeable audience. Luckily, the solution is available to everyone; great storytelling. Write on a breakout scale and you can make it. Many of my clients have; you can too.

—*Donald Maass, literary agent and author of* The Career Novelist, Writing the Breakout Novel *and* Writing the Breakout Novel Workbook

Chincoteague
~Cedar Gables Seaside Inn
Located in a quiet neighborhood, this four-room bed and breakfast inn has water and marshland views and some of the rooms have private spa tubs. All have private baths, TV/VCR, data ports, and individualized furnishings. There is a boat dock and breakfast is included in the room price.

> 6095 Hopkins Lane, Chincoteague, VA 23336
> 757-336-6860
> $$$–$$$$

Norfolk
~Bed & Breakfast At the Page House Inn
Situated in the historic district of town, this Georgian Revival mansion was renovated in 1990, and all the seven rooms are decorated with natural woods and antique furnishings and have private baths, hair dryers, modern amenities, data ports, and some units have spa tubs. Small pets are okay. Breakfast is included.

323 Fairfax Ave., Norfolk, VA 23507
757-625-5033
$$$–$$$$

THE MORE THE BETTER

It's a tough market out there. You want to cover all bases when you are in search of work. I usually suggest hauling a portfolio of twelve to fifteen pieces to personally show art directors and editors. I feel it is important for them to "see the face behind the work."

When I started my career, I made two trips a year to New York to meet with publishers and keep in contact. As for the portfolio pieces, I took a wide assortment of work. I figured that I wanted to give myself the best opportunity to get an assignment. There were pieces that showed I could draw and paint kids both inside and outdoors, a painting showing a child in motion, animals both anthropomorphic and more realistic, a few pieces showing how I would handle fairy tales and folk tales, a black and white rendering of something nonfictional that would be applicable for young adult novels, pieces showing a sense of humor, and the rest showing the kind of work I was most interested in—wildlife.

Always make sure that all the art you show a publisher is geared towards children's books if that is what you wish to illustrate. Don't show old college projects—it will turn them off.

—*Daniel San Souci, award-winning children's book illustrator and author*

Richmond
~*The Jefferson Hotel*

This large, historic hotel located right in downtown, has 264 rooms, and this landmark 1895 Beaux Arts hotel is a magnificent piece of architecture, with its grand staircase, statue of Thomas Jefferson, and stained glass rotunda. Even if you don't stay here, just visit the lobby. There are one-bedroom suites, some with spa tubs, and all rooms have private baths, data ports, safes, hair dryers, and all the modern amenities and business services. There is a heated pool, restaurant, and bar.

101 W. Franklin St., Richmond, VA 23220
866-247-2303

www.Jefferson-hotel.com
$$$$$

Stephens City
~Inn at Vaucluse Spring

This unusual and bucolic inn at the northern end of the Shenandoah Valley near Shenandoah National Park is set among 100 acres of hills and orchards. It contains several cottages with fifteen rooms and suites, including a 200-year-old manor house. Some rooms have views of the mountains or the Vaucluse Springs. Rooms are luxuriously appointed, with fireplaces, private baths with some spa tubs, and a full breakfast is included.

231 Vaucluse Springs Lane, Stephens City, VA 22655
800-869-0525
www.vauclusespring.com
$$–$$$$$

Virginia Beach
~Barclay Cottage Bed & Breakfast

This historic turn-of-the-century inn was formerly a schoolhouse and is now a six-room bed and breakfast, located by the beach, but in a quiet residential neighborhood a little away from the main distractions of the beach strip. There are some shared baths, but the rooms are comfortable and clean and the wraparound veranda is a wonderful spot for reflection.

400 16th St., Virginia Beach, VA 23451
757-422-1956
$–$$$

~The Dunes Oceanfront

Located on the quieter south side of the city, this hotel has 107 one-bedroom units with kitchenettes. It is right on the beach and every room has a private terrace facing the ocean. Accommodations are average and motel-like, with private baths, coffee, and there is a heated pool. There are discounts available for extended stays.

921 Atlantic Ave., Virginia Beach, VA 23451
800-634-0709

www.thedunesoceanfront.com
$–$$$$

North Carolina

Asheville
~Richmond Hill Inn
The gorgeous Blue Ridge Parkway and Mountains provide numerous scenic destinations, but some of the loveliest are right in Asheville. This Asheville mansion, high up on a hill, has rooms in the mansion, as well as individual cottages. There are 33 rooms total—all with private baths. Each room is luxurious and has antique furnishings. Some rooms have fireplaces or porches with rocking chairs and views of hills, waterfalls, and gardens. There is a library and fine restaurant in the mansion. Breakfast and tea are included.

87 Richmond Hill Dr., Asheville, NC 28806
888-742-4550
www.richmondhillinn.com/
$$$–$$$$$

~Albemarle Inn
This historic turn-of-the-century Southern mansion is close to the historic downtown, yet a world away, with its elegant oak staircase and parlor rooms and large, stone veranda. All eleven rooms have private baths with clawfoot tubs, fine linens, fresh flowers, robes, and luxurious amenities. A hearty breakfast, afternoon tea, and refreshments are served with total Southern hospitality.

86 Edgemont Rd., Asheville, NC 28801
800-621-7435
www.albemarleinn.com
$$$–$$$$$

Bald Head Island
~Marsh Harbour Inn
Located at the southeastern tip of North Carolina, this island has a New

England-style inn right in the village at the harbor. The only way to get to the island is by ferry from Southport. Rooms at the inn have hardwood floors, private baths, shaker beds, TV, phones, Cape Cod rockers, and decks with water views. Breakfast and golf are included. House rentals are also available and vary but from one to five bedrooms, containing fully furnished kitchens and furnishings.

5079 Southport-Supply Rd., Southport, NC 28461
800-432-RENT
www.Baldheadisland.com
$$–$$$$

Richmond Hill Inn, Asheville, NC. The Mansion's wood-paneled parlor is perfect for reading, writing, or partaking in the daily afternoon tea and pastries served there. Courtesy of Richmond Hill Inn

Hendersonville
~The Waverly Inn
Located just twenty miles south of Asheville in the southern Blue Ridge Mountains, this bed and breakfast is the oldest inn in the historic part of

Hendersonville. Listed on the National Historic Register, the inn has thirteen rooms and one suite, all with private baths and all with period pieces, four-poster beds, natural woodworking, cable TV, and high-speed Internet access. There is a library and a porch with wicker rocking chairs. Breakfast and afternoon refreshments are included.

783 N. Main St., Hendersonville, NC 28792
800-537-8195
www.waverlyinn.com
$$–$$$$

Kitty Hawk
~Bald View Bed & Breakfast
Located on the outer banks, this 4-room inn has comfortable rooms on expansive grounds with views of the bay, about five minutes from the ocean. All rooms have private baths, and a light breakfast is included in the room price.

3805 Elijah Baum Rd., Kitty Hawk, NC 27949
252-255-2829
www.baldview.com
$$–$$$

Lake Toxaway
~Greystone Inn
Listed on the National Historic Register, this 33-room hotel on beautiful Lake Toxaway, makes you feel you've fallen into a fairy tale.

The six-story Swiss-style mansion was built in 1915, but renovated in 1985. Henry Ford, Thomas Edison, and the Rockefellers stayed here. Rooms are beautiful, with canopied or brass beds, fireplaces, private baths, and balconies with mountain or lake views. There is a library and a porch with wicker furniture, and boating activities are included, but you must work hard to stay focused here. Breakfast, dinner, and afternoon tea are included and the food is excellent.

Greystone Lane, Lake Toxaway, NC 28747
800-824-5766
www.greystoneinn.com
$$$$$

Nag's Head

~First Colony Inn

Listed on the National Register of Historic Places, this charming inn has 26 rooms, all with private baths, some with spa tubs, and four are efficiencies with kitchenettes. Rooms have coffee, refrigerators, grills, picnic tables, and a full breakfast is included. A pool is located on the premises.

> 6720 S. Virginia Dare Trail, Nag's Head NC 27947
> 800-368-9390
> www.firstcolonyinn.com
> $–$$$$$

Waynesville

~The Swag Country Inn

Deep in the Great Smoky Mountains National Park, this great country inn on 250 acres is at an altitude of 5,000 feet on top of a mountain. There are twelve rooms and three suites, all furnished beautifully and differently with original arts and crafts from the area, and the rooms all have feather beds, fireplaces, balconies with astounding views, and steam showers. This inn has won many awards, and meals, as well as afternoon tea, are included.

> 2300 Swag Rd., Waynesville, NC 28785
> 800-789-7672
> www.theswag.com
> $$$$$

THE
SOUTHEAST

South Carolina

Georgia

Florida

Alabama

Mississippi

Louisiana

Southern hospitality is usually evident at all lodgings in the southeast region of the country. Don't forget to take in the lush, magnificent foliage as well as the miles of exquisite coastline. And, be sure to indulge in the sinful and divine southern cuisine.

South Carolina

Charleston

~Two Meeting Street Inn

Located in one of the most charming cities in the country, this nine-room romantic Queen Anne Victorian stands out as one of the prettiest buildings in town. Located in the historic district, the rockers on the arched veranda look out over the Charleston Battery. All rooms have private baths, elegant antique furnishings, canopy beds, Tiffany windows, and high ceilings. An expanded continental breakfast, afternoon tea, and refreshments are included in the room price.

> 2 Meeting St., Charleston, SC 29401
> 843-723-7322
> www.twomeetingstreet.com
> $$$–$$$$$

~Governor's House Inn

This is the former governor's mansion, located in the historical district and built in the 1700s, is an elegant and comfortable inn with eleven rooms and suites. All rooms have private baths, some with spa tubs and fireplaces, high ceilings, antique furnishings, and canopy beds. Some rooms have private porches, and the common rooms have original fireplaces, oriental rugs, chandeliers, and period pieces. Continental breakfast and afternoon tea are included.

> 117 Broad St., Charleston, SC 29401
> 800-720-9812
> www.governorshouse.com
> $$$–$$$$$

Conway
~The Cypress Inn

Located near Myrtle Beach, this twelve-room inn overlooks a marina, and some rooms have water views. All rooms are uniquely furnished, have private baths, some with spa tubs, some with fireplaces, and all have TV/VCR, air conditioning, robes, and fine linens. Breakfast is included in the room price.

> 16 Elm St., Conway, SC 29526
> 800-575-5307
> www.acypressinn.com
> $$–$$$$

Pawleys Island
~Litchfield Plantation

This is the place for *Gone With the Wind* fans. This former rice-growing plantation on 600 acres on the South Carolina coast, was built in the 1750s and is truly a Southern plantation. Only 25 miles south of Myrtle Beach, the driveway is a quarter of a mile of live oaks overlapping each other across the road, and there is a pool, tennis courts, library and restaurant. Continental breakfast is included. All the rooms have private baths, cable TV, data ports, luxurious décor, and range from regular rooms to suites with lake views, kitchenettes in the villas, and elegant amenities.

> P.O. Box 290, Kings River Rd., Pawleys Island, SC 29585
> 800-869-1410
> www.litchfieldplantation.com
> $$$–$$$$$

Georgia

Georgia is one of those states that has something for everyone, from a major city like Atlanta, to beaches and ocean and mountains and lakes. From Atlanta heading north to the north Georgia mountains at the bottom of the Appalachian chain, you will find numerous small, quaint towns and wineries.

Blairsville
~Arkaquah Valley Inn
Located about two hours from Atlanta, Chattanooga, or Knoxville, this bed and breakfast has four rooms with private baths, sitting areas, feather beds, comforters and quilts. Situated next to the Chattahoochee National Forest in the Blue Ridge Mountains, the inn's rooms have views of the surrounding wilderness, and common rooms have stained glass and fireplaces. Breakfast is included.

> 5146 Trackrock Camp Rd., Blairsville, GA 30512
> 706-745-9182
> www.arkaquahvalleyinn.com
> $–$$

Clarkesville
~Glen-Ella Springs Inn
Located at the edge of the Blue Ridge Mountains on eighteen acres, this bed and breakfast is on the National Register of Historic Places. The sixteen-room inn has charming rooms with wood paneling, local handcrafted pieces, private baths, air conditioning, phones, and porches with lovely garden and hill views. There is an outdoor pool and a sundeck, and a hearty breakfast is included, although dinners are extra.

> 1789 Bear Gap Rd., Clarkesville, GA 30523
> 888-455-8896
> www.glenella.com
> $$–$$$$

Helen
~The Lodge at Unicoi
Located less than two hours north of Atlanta and in one of the over 60 parks and historic sites operated by the state's park service, this charming lodge is right in the park, high up on a mountain overlooking waterfalls. The lodge rooms have all the basic amenities and there are private cottages with kitchenettes and wood burning stoves. Bed and bath linens are provided, but there are no televisions or phones.

> 1788 Hwy 356, PO Box 849, Helen, GA 30545
> 800-864-7275
> $–$$$

Sautee

~Lucille's Mountain Top Inn

Located about 90 minutes north of Atlanta, this bed and breakfast sits on top of a mountain in the north Georgia hills in the Sautee Valley. All rooms have wonderful views, contemporary furnishings with ceiling fans, TV/VCR, robes, hair dryers, private baths, some with spa tubs and fireplaces, desks with data ports, voice mail, and other business services. A large breakfast and evening dessert and beverages are included and served on the back porch, overlooking the valley below.

> 964 Rabun Rd., Sautee, GA 30571
> 866-245-4777
> www.lucillesmountaintopinn.com
> $$$–$$$$

Atlanta

~The Georgian Terrace Hotel

In the early twentieth century, this grand hotel was called the city's "Parisian hotel" since it looked more like a fine European hotel than a Southern one. A $10-million renovation in 2001 kept the original grandeur of the 1911 building, but added high-speed Internet access, upscale suites with kitchens, a new restaurants, and a 19-story glass atrium lobby that reflects the original mosaic tile floor. The 319 rooms all have private baths, luxurious amenities, and city views. The hotel offers a pool, fitness center, and business services, as well as room service.

> 659 Peachtree St., Atlanta, GA 30308
> 800-651-2316
> www.thegeorgianterrace.com
> $$$$–$$$$$

Greenville

~Grand Wisteria Plantation Bed & Breakfast

Located just 50 minutes southwest of Atlanta, this six-room, 1832-plantation manor house sits on 13 acres of beautiful grounds and gardens. It is on the National Register of Historic Places and all the rooms are beautifully-appointed, with antiques and private baths. Breakfast and wine and cordials are included.

15380 Roosevelt Hwy., Greenville, GA 30222
706-672-0072
www.grandwisteria.com
$$–$$$

Palmetto
~Serenbe Bed and Breakfast Farm
This turn-of-the-century inn on 350 acres has over 100 animals, three streams, two waterfalls, a swimming pool and a lake. Located only 32 miles from Atlanta, this peaceful ten-room farm has three unique buildings with some guest rooms in each. All have private baths and some have spa tubs. Rooms contain antique Southern folk art, and some have sitting areas or reading nooks with lake views. Rates include full breakfast, afternoon and evening refreshments. No credit cards.

10950 Hutcheson Ferry Rd., Palmetto, GA 30268
770-463-2610
www.serenbe.com
$$$

Macon
~1842 Inn
This award-winning bed and breakfast dates from 1842 and boasts white pillars and large porch. The 21 rooms have private baths, some with spa tubs and fireplaces, all with elegant antique furnishings and artwork, and turn-down service. Breakfast and afternoon refreshments are included.

353 College St., Macon, GA 31201
800-336-1842
www.the1842inn.com
$$$–$$$$

Watkinsville
~Ashford Manor
Located just south of Athens, home of the University of Georgia, this beautiful and bucolic 1893 Victorian bed and breakfast sits on five acres of well-manicured grounds and gardens. The five rooms have private baths, air conditioning, all the basic amenities, and period furnishings with vintage town photographs. Breakfast is included and dogs are allowed.

5 Harden Hill Rd., Watkinsville, GA 30677
706-769-2633
www.ambedandbreakfast.com
$–$$$

Savannah

~*Magnolia Place Inn*

Located at Forsyth Park, this magnificent Victorian was built in 1878 and is in the historic district of charming Savannah. With thirteen rooms in the mansion and two row houses available, all the accommodations are elegant, with private baths, some with spa tubs, canopy or four-poster beds, fabulous European antiques throughout, fireplaces, and a parlor and porches overlooking the lovely park. Breakfast, afternoon tea, refreshments, beverages and port are included.

503 Whitaker St., Savannah, GA 31401
800-238-7674
www.magnoliaplaceinn.com
$$$–$$$$$

~*The President's Quarters*

This Federal-style mansion built in the 1850s overlooks Oglethorpe Square and is close to the historic district and only a short ride to the ocean. The eleven rooms and eight suites are large and luxuriously appointed, with magnificent antique furnishings, fine linens, oriental rugs, fireplaces, canopy or four-poster beds, high ceilings, desks with data ports, TV/VCR, private baths, and some have spa tubs, steam showers, balconies, or sitting rooms. A full breakfast and an afternoon reception are included.

225 E. President St., Savannah, GA 31401
800-233-1776
www.presidentsquarters.com
$$$–$$$$$

~*The Manor House*

This waterfront inn with five rooms was built in 1840 as a cotton broker's office. All rooms have private baths and the suite has a spa tub, private entrance, and fireplace. All the rooms are furnished individually with fine fabrics and linens and period pieces, and all have canopy beds. Continental breakfast is included and served in the parlor. Small pets are okay.

> 201 W. Liberty St., Savannah, GA 31401
> 800-462-3595
> www.manorhouse-savannah.com
> $$$$$

PROPOSE A BOOK

It's been said the best view for a writer is a brick wall. Just going to another city will help. Try this when you need to concentrate on writing a nonfiction book proposal.

Although there is no one way to write a proposal, any more than there is one way to write a book, the following technique has evolved over the last thirty years. It's the fastest, easiest way I know of to make your proposal rejection-proof and get the best editor, publisher, and deal for your book.

Most proposals range from thirty to fifty pages. Your title must tell and sell the book. Each part of your proposal must convince agents and editors to go on to the next part. Here are the three parts of a proposal: the introduction, the outline and the sample chapter. Create as much excitement as you can about yourself and your book. The goals of the introduction are to prove that you have a solid, marketable idea and that you are the right person to write and promote it. The introduction has three parts: overview, resources needed to complete the book, and About the Author.

For the outline, write about the chapters, not about the subject. You must prove that there is a book's worth of information in your idea and that you have devised the best structure for organizing it. Write from a paragraph to a page of prose outlining each chapter. Aim for one line of outline for every page of text. For example, write nineteen lines of outline for a nineteen-page chapter. Start each chapter outline with the strongest anecdote or slice of copy from that chapter, and then do the outline.

The sample chapter should be as enjoyable to read as it is enlightening. Choose the strongest representative chapter that will best show how well you write.

—*Michael Larsen, literary agent (Larsen-Pomada Literary Agents) and author of several books on publishing and* Guerrilla Marketing for Writers

Florida

The Sunshine state's main industry is tourism and there are thousands of places to stay in this large and beautiful state, blessed with thousands of miles of oceanfront. Listed here are some of my favorite places, perfect for creative folks.

The Keys

Islamorada
~Pelican Cove Resort

Some of the best room views in Florida are to be found at this modern inn. There are rooms, efficiencies with kitchenettes and suites, and all have private baths and private balconies. There is a pool, spa, beach, pier, outdoor bar and café, all on the oceanfront with wonderful views of egrets flying over the turquoise water of the cove in front of the hotel. Writing at the picnic tables on the beach is delightful.

> 84457 Old Overseas Hwy., Islamorada, FL 33036
> 800-445-4690
> www.pcove.com
> $$–$$$$$

Key Largo
~Coconut Palm Inn

This beachfront hideaway fronts the Florida Bay and has sixteen rooms and suites, most with water views, all with private baths, phones, air conditioning, coffee, refrigerators, cable TV, and porches or decks, and the suites have kitchens. There is a pool, hammocks, private docks, BBQs and 400 feet of sandy beach. A complimentary continental breakfast is served.

> 198 Harborview Dr., Key Largo, FL 33070
> 800-765-5397
> www.coconutpalminn.com
> $$–$$$$$

BE A FRIEND

Because writing is such a solitary occupation, I think it's important to brush up those social skills every so often and spend time with the people you care about. If they are truly good friends, they'll be interested in your progress, happy when you are on a roll, and sympathetic when the words won't come. They will know how to take no for an answer, a virtue appreciated by every writer on a deadline. They will be supportive and they will want success for you, almost as much as you want it yourself. If you have family and friends who exhibit these traits, treasure them. And remember what my granny used to say: You have to be a friend to have a friend.

—*Karen Jones Delk, author of six novels*

~Heron House

This small, luxurious hotel actually sits on a gorgeous courtyard, with pool and gardens. The 23 rooms, located in three buildings, are all individualized and have private baths, phone, air conditioning, cable TV, and some are located at poolside. There are suites available and an orchid nursery is on the premises. The hotel is only one block from the main street of shops and restaurants and Ernest Hemingway's house in the historic district. Breakfast and a wine reception in the afternoon are included.

512 Simonton St., Key West, FL 33040
888-265-2395
www.heronhouse.com
$$–$$$$$

North and Central Florida

Amelia Island
~Elizabeth Pointe Lodge

Located at the northern part of Florida, near the Georgia border, this New-England-style bed and breakfast sits right on the beach, and all 24 rooms are waterfront, with private baths that include large soaking tubs. Complimentary refreshments are served throughout the day and a large veranda make this a heavenly spot.

> 98 S. Fletcher Ave. (A1A), Amelia Island, FL 32034
> 888-757-1910
> www.elizabethpointelodge.com
> **$$$–$$$$$**

Longboat Key
~The Colony Beach & Tennis Resort

On the west coast of Florida on the Gulf of Mexico, Long Boat Key you will find one of the nation's prettiest locations, and this large hotel has wonderful views and facilities right on the beach. The 234 rooms are elegantly appointed suites, with one-or two-bedrooms and private, marble baths with spa tubs or steam showers. Suites have living rooms, full kitchenettes, data ports, and balconies. There is a spa and business services are available, along with restaurants, a lounge, pools, and full recreational activities.

> 1620 Gulf of Mexico Dr., Longboat Key, FL 34228
> 941-383-6464
> www.thecolony.com
> **$$$$–$$$$$**

Orlando
~Eo Inn

This former YMCA building, restored from the 1920s, is now a boutique hotel with cozy, but plush, modern rooms with private baths facing Lake Eola, and some rooms have lake views. The inn is located in the Thornton Park neighborhood, and all the rooms are "smart" rooms, with high tech services available for business. There are also hair dryers and CD players in each room. Spa services are available.

> 227 N. Eola Drive, Orlando, FL 32801
> 888-481-8488
> www.eoinn.com
> **$$$–$$$$**

South Florida

Deerfield Beach
~Rettger Resorts Beach Club
Situated at a perfect location across from one of the safest and prettiest beaches in South Florida, this basic two-story motel-like inn has standard rooms, as well as suites and studios with kitchenettes. All rooms have private baths, beautiful ocean views, and a continental breakfast is included. A pool overlooks the Atlantic Ocean. Special rates for extended stays are available. Several ocean view restaurants are located steps away, as well as a fishing pier.

> 100 N.E. 20th Terrace, Deerfield Beach, FL 33441
> 888-738-8437
> www.RettgerResorts.com
> $-$$$

Miami Beach
~Delano Hotel
This is an Ian Schrager hotel, built in 1995 on the ocean in Miami Beach. Rooms are modern, with high-speed Internet access, all with private baths, most have ocean views, and all have cable TV, hair dryers, safes, and include room service. The specially designed pool has underwater music, and there is a rooftop spa/solarium.

> 1685 Collins Ave, Miami Beach, FL 33139
> 305-672-2000
> $$$$$

Palm Beach
~The Breakers
Since 1896, this oceanfront resort has been a playground for the wealthy. Set on 140 acres right along the beach, the resort offers 560 rooms (57 are suites), with every luxurious amenity imaginable, including private marble baths, Italian armoires, safes, robes, high-speed Internet access, dual phones and data ports, fine linens, and many have balconies with ocean views. There are four pools, spas, a fitness center, tennis courts, two golf courses, shops, restaurants and bars. The grounds are beautifully manicured and there are many places to sit and write.

One South County Rd., Palm Beach, FL 33480
888-273-2537
www.thebreakers.com
$$$$$

Sanibel Island

~Royal Shell Vacations

This oceanfront resort is located on The Gulf Coast, in one of the love-liest beaches in Florida. The rooms here are comfortable, motel-like, and have private baths. It's the ocean views and wonderful beach that make it special. The entire island and Captiva Island next to it, via a small bridge, are wonderful escapes.

1200 Periwinkle Dr., Sanibel, FL 33957
800-396-1885
www.onlinhotels.com/Sanibel
$$–$$$$

Alabama

Jemison

~The Jemison Inn

Located between Birmingham and Montgomery, this charming bed and breakfast has three unique rooms, all with private baths (one with a clawfoot tub, one with a spa tub), fresh flowers, cable TV/VCR, and robes. There is a pool and lovely gardens with fountains. Breakfast and afternoon refreshments are complimentary. All rooms are located on the main floor.

212 Highway 191, Jemison, AL 35085
205-688-2055
www.bbonline.com/al/Jemison/
$

Lincoln

~The Governor's House

This historic bed and breakfast was built in 1850 by a former Alabama governor. In 1990, it was moved to a farm, renovated, and now there are three guestrooms with private baths and one with a shared bath. There is also a barn room with a front porch. All rooms have air conditioning, antiques, quilts, ceiling fans, fruit and flowers. A full breakfast and afternoon refreshments are included and there is a pond and boat rides are available on Logan Martin Lake next to the inn.

> 500 Meadowlake Lane, Talladega, AL 35160
> 205-763-2186
> $$

Orange Beach
~The Original Romar House
Alabama's first seaside inn, established in 1924, is located right on Romar Beach, east of Gulf Shores. There are five individually appointed rooms, one suite, and one cottage, all with private baths and period furnishings. The Purple Parrot Bar, overlooking the Gulf of Mexico, offers complimentary drinks and cheese for guests. Breakfast is also included.

> 23500 Perdido Beach Blvd., Orange Beach, AL 36561
> 800-487-6627
> www.bbonline.com/al/romarhouse/
> $-$$$

Mississippi

Biloxi
~Green Oaks
This bed and breakfast, built in 1826, is Mississippi's oldest beachfront mansion. The five rooms are beautifully appointed, with period furnishings, private baths, and air conditioning. A gourmet breakfast is included in the room price.

> 580 Beach Blvd., Biloxi, MS 39530
> 888-436-6257
> $$-$$$

Natchez
~Dunleith Plantation

Located on 40 well-manicured acres, this white colonnade-style historic inn has 26 rooms, all with private baths and eleven with spa tubs. All rooms are individually decorated, with period and reproduction pieces, and all have air conditioning, cable TV, robes, phones, and fireplaces. A full breakfast is included and the inn is known for its wonderful restaurant.

84 Homochitts St., Natchez, MS 39204
800-433-2445
www.dunleithplantation.com
$$$–$$$$$

JUST THE BASICS

For me, there's a creative release that comes with writing in a new place. There's something exciting about being away from home and all its distractions. I need a clean room with a comfortable chair, a desk, and a bed with a good mattress. A window with an interesting view and good light is important, and an easily accessible place to walk is essential.

—*Elissa Haden Guest, author of novels and children's books*

~Monmouth Plantation

This antebellum plantation is a National Historic Landmark, built in the early 1800s. Situated on 26 magnificent acres of gardens and ponds, the inn offers 15 rooms and 16 suites, scattered among five buildings, including the main mansion. All rooms are filled with elegant antiques and art and have private baths and modern amenities. A full breakfast is included and there is a restaurant on the premises.

36 Melrose Ave., Natchez, MS 39120
800-828-4531
www.monmouthplantation.com
$$$–$$$$$

Louisiana

Napoleonville
~Madewood Plantation House

This magnificent plantation house located, west of New Orleans, consists of six rooms and two suites, all with private baths, antique furnishings, and canopy beds. This award-winning country inn has beautiful grounds and the kitchen is renowned for the cuisine (meals are extra).

> 4250 Hwy 308, Napoleonville, LA 70390
> 800-375-7151
> www.madewood.com
> $$$$–$$$$$

CREATE MAGIC

New Orleans is my favorite place. Just the experience of being there for several days—the weather—the lighting—the energy of the place—it has a feeling of magic and voodoo and that anything could happen. It's a little amoral and, if you could have an affair and get away with it, here is where it would happen. Walk around and absorb the atmosphere to generate creativity. Eat fun foods, such as beignets and coffee or bananas foster.

—*Stephanie Lurie, president and publisher of Dutton Children's Books, a division of the PenguinGroup*

New Orleans
~The Lafayette Hotel

Located near the convention center and a short walk to the French Quarter, this small, luxurious hotel has 44 elegant rooms and suites, with private baths that include marble tubs, fine fabrics, robes, air conditioning, and French doors with wrought iron balconies, all providing charm and comfort. The magnificent lobby is decorated with mahogany furniture and Italian marble.

600 St. Charles Ave., New Orleans, LA 70130
888-856-4706
www.thelafayettehotel.com
$$$–$$$$$

~Hotel Maison De Ville

Located in the historic French Quarter of the city, this beautiful and charming inn has 23 rooms and some separate cottages. There is a court-yard, with fountains and a pool. All the rooms have private baths, four-poster or canopy beds, fine art, and elegant antique furnishings. Breakfast and sherry are included in the room price.

727 Rue Toulouse, New Orleans, LA 70130
800-634-1600
www.maisondeville.com
$$$$–$$$$$

Index by Venue

Index by City

About the Author

Andrea Brown formed her literary agency in 1981. Formerly an editor at Alfred A. Knopf, she has sold more than 1,000 books to just about every publisher. Brown is a regular speaker at numerous writers conferences. She has published many articles; been interviewed in *Forbes, Good Housekeeping,* and *Writer's Digest;* appeared on C-Span's "Book Notes;" and is executive director of the Big Sur Writing Workshops for children's books and adult fiction.

More great Quill Driver Books' titles on writing & publishing!

$29.95 ($45.00 *Canada*)
- ISBN 1-884956-40-8
(Replaces 3rd Edition, ISBN 1-884956-19-X)
- Indexed by topics

The American Directory of
Writer's Guidelines, 4th Edition
A Compilation of Information for Freelancers from More than 1,500 Magazine Editors and Book Publishers

—Compiled and Edited by Brigitte M. Phillips, Susan D. Klassen and Doris Hall

Perhaps the best-kept secret in the publishing industry is that many publishers—both periodical publishers and book publishers—make available writer's guidelines to assist would-be contributors. Written by the staff at each publishing house, these guidelines help writers target their submissions to the exact needs of the individual publisher. *The American Directory of Writer's Guidelines* is a compilation of the actual writer's guidelines for more than 1,500 publishers.

❝*Unlike the entries in Writer's Market (Writer's Digest, annual), which edits the information supplied by publishers and prints it in a standard entry format, this new resource contains unedited self-descriptions of publications and publishing houses.*❞
—Booklist

$14.95 ($22.50 *Canada*)
- ISBN 1-884956-17-3

Damn! Why Didn't I Write That?

How Ordinary People are Raking in $100,000.00... Or More Writing Nonfiction Books & How You Can Too!

—by Marc McCutcheon

A Book-of-the-Month Club, Quality Paperback Book Club, and Writer's Digest Book Club Selection!

More nonfiction books are breaking the 100,000-copy sales barrier than ever before. Amateur writers, housewives, and even high school dropouts have cashed in with astonishingly simple best-sellers. This guide, by best-selling author Marc McCutcheon, shows the reader how to get in on the action.

❝*Comprehensive and engaging this book will save you time, energy, and frustration.*❞
—Michael Larsen, literary agent, author

Available at better brick and mortar bookstores, online bookstores, at QuillDriverBooks.com or by calling toll-free 1-800-497-4909